VICTORY AT RISK

VICTORY AT RISK

Restoring America's Military Power:
A New War Plan for the Pentagon

MAJOR GENERAL
MICHAEL W. DAVIDSON
U.S. ARMY (RET.)

ZENITH PRESS

First published in 2009 by Zenith Press, an imprint of MBI Publishing Company, 400 1st Avenue North, Suite 300, Minneapolis, MN 55401 USA.

Zenith Press titles are also available at discounts in bulk quantity for industrial or sales-promotional use. For details write to Special Sales Manager at MBI Publishing Company, 400 1st Avenue North, Suite 300, Minneapolis, MN 55401 USA.

To find out more about our books, join us online at www.zenithpress.com.

Library of Congress Cataloging-in-Publication Data

Davidson, Michael W., 1947-
 Victory at risk : restoring America's military power : a new war plan for the Pentagon / Major General Michael W. Davidson, U.S. Army (Ret.).
    p. cm.
  ISBN 978-0-7603-3557-4 (hbk.)
  1. United States—Armed Forces—Operational readiness. 2. United States. Dept. of Defense—Reorganization. 3. United States—Armed Forces—Reorganization. 4. Civil-military relations—United States. 5. United States—Military policy. 6. Strategic culture—United States. 7. United States—History, Military. I. Title.
  UA23.D2755 2009
  355'.033573—dc22
                    2008036563

Front cover image: *Lawrence Lawry/Getty Images*

Designer: Diana Boger

Printed in the United States of America

To the men and women currently serving in uniform.

To them we owe our freedom;

to our freedom we owe all else that we have.

Contents

Preface

I LEARNED TO BE A SOLDIER in one night. The army spent the better part of two years training me—infantry training, infantry officer candidate school, airborne training, Special Forces training—but it was a single night in Vietnam when I learned the real parts of soldiering.

I volunteered for Vietnam. One too many Special Forces sergeants glanced condescendingly at my uniform, which bore no combat badges. I borrowed a jeep that was not locked up, drove off the mountain from the field training exercise I was on, and called infantry branch at the Pentagon to volunteer. I called from a pay phone. When the assignments officer I was talking to figured out that I was putting fistfuls of coins in the phone to volunteer for a combat tour, he took pity on a green lieutenant and got me on a plane to Vietnam.

The personnel section of the 1st Air Cavalry Division at Bien Hoa was having trouble filling a lieutenant's billet in their Ranger Company. I should have asked why but, having more bravado than sense, I asked for the job and got it. The mission of the Ranger Company was to send five- or six-man patrols—four or five Americans and one hopefully former Viet Cong—on long-range reconnaissance missions. We went in well away from any other friendly forces—in fact they put a one-kilometer buffer zone around our four-kilometer area of operations. I never knew whether that was to protect us from everyone else or to protect everyone else from us.

On each mission that I was on, we flagrantly broke a basic army rule. Rank within the patrol was not based on the rank the army gave you; it was based on the number of missions you had completed and how well you had done. My commission designating me an officer and a gentleman, my Special Forces tab, and my jump wings all amounted to nothing. I began my combat tour as a radio operator for a buck sergeant team leader. In the rear area, I was a lieutenant, but Ranger Company officers were not supposed to go on patrols. If you wanted to do that, you started at the bottom and worked your way up.

On one of those patrols, late in the afternoon in some very dense jungle, my team leader spotted tracks on a muddy bank across a sizable stream. There was no one there then, but a lot of people had recently been there. We stayed on our side of the stream, hidden as well as we could manage as darkness fell.

My sergeant had it nailed. We had stumbled on a sampan docking site, a place where people off-loaded from one set of boats and got on another. That night, we watched over a hundred North Vietnamese and Viet Cong make camp across the stream from us. They were very close, and I practiced lying in the jungle as quietly as anyone ever had. The Vietnamese left on another set of sampans before the sun came up. In the morning, my sergeant decided that we should move to their side of the stream and set up an ambush for the next group coming through. All six of us.

We crossed the stream and set up a claymore anti-personnel mine ambush and then hid in the center of their camp. That night, another group of Vietnamese came through. We blew the ambush and lay still, hoping they would think it was an unmanned mechanical ambush. After a few minutes, people who had not been in the kill zone began to move about. We threw hand grenades in the direction of the sound of the movement, more death from out of the night from who knew what direction.

This mission had become a big deal for the 1st Cav. We had helicopter gunships hovering beyond a line of hills to mask their noise. When we blew the claymores, the gunships came on station within minutes, firing machine guns, 40mm cannons and rockets. American helicopter pilots can and will fire very close if the ground commander authorizes it. They call it "danger close," and that captures the sense of the thing.

The gunships eventually ran low on fuel and the Brigade operations officer—a ferocious colonel with the confidence-inspiring call sign Fang—ordered our team out of the area. That would be a challenge. There was no place to land a helicopter where we were, and there were too many of the enemy about for us to run. So we did something called a McGuire rig extraction. It's a simple concept: a Huey hovers over the jungle at something lower than one hundred feet and drops three or four ropes with one end still tied to the helicopter. You put your legs through a loop at your end of the rope, hold on, and they lift you out. As the first of the two helicopters pulled us out, our Vietnamese scout inadvertently got a rope longer than the others and was sure that we were leaving him. He grabbed for me as we lifted off and I carried him for the flight back. We left just in time. One of the gunships landed at the nearest fire base with what he estimated was two minutes of fuel left on board his aircraft.

When dawn came, the Brigade commander gave us reinforcements and we went back into the jungle. We said it was to gather intelligence—and we did in fact do that—but the truth was that we wanted to see how many of the enemy we had killed. It was that kind of war.

We found a lot of bodies. Even more parts of bodies. The two junior members of the Ranger team, me being one, were tasked with stripping the dead and putting the personal effects in waterproof bags for the Brigade intelligence section to process. The events of the night before had been wrought with fear and felt something like a movie; the early morning light let me see what war was really about.

Here is what I learned that night.

It is OK to be afraid. Anyone with any sense is afraid in combat. Courage is being able to do your job even though you are afraid.

Good combat soldiers may or may not outrank the people they are, or should be, ordering about. God love my team sergeant—every lieutenant should have such a sergeant while he is figuring out how wars are fought. All the way through becoming a general, I never got to be as good a soldier as that sergeant was.

Soldering is an honorable calling. If it has to be done, it should be done well. But we should try very hard to keep from unnecessarily sending our soldiers in harm's way. Their lives are too valuable to waste.

Introduction

AMERICA'S FUTURE MILITARY VICTORIES are at risk. We proudly portray ourselves as the world's sole superpower, yet America has stretched its army to the breaking point sustaining a modestly sized counterinsurgency in Iraq. The United States spends more on defense than the next dozen nations in the world combined, but has an army that is at meager pre–Pearl Harbor force levels.[1] For two centuries, the United States won every war that it fought. We then went from victory in World War II to stalemate in Korea to defeat in Vietnam to a strategic misadventure in Iraq. Our current ability to fight and win the nation's wars is at best suspect. We have allowed the bedrock sources of our past success to erode due to misuse, atrophy, and neglect.

America wins wars when we go to war for compelling causes and when military and civilian leaders of strategic vision emerge. America wins wars when the ranks of our military are filled with citizen soldiers. They are the strength of the nation, and they take America to war with them. That kind of military strength cannot be purchased: there are no American Hessians. America wins wars when all of America goes to war. Our power lies in our ideals, in our economy, and in the commitment of our people more than in formations of soldiers and fleets of ships and airplanes. America wins wars when our values are intact and are honored, values shared between our citizens and our soldiers. Those values guide our soldiers in the chaos of combat and allow our senior military officers to advise civilian leaders forthrightly on crucial go-to-war decisions. America wins wars when we go to war

1

to defend freedom. Our country was founded on the simple idea that people are and should be free. When that freedom has been challenged, America has gone to war and found victory. When we go to war for other reasons, we fare less well.

Today, we have drifted from the sources of our past success. Presidents now send standing military forces off to war with little involvement—and even less commitment—from the American public. We chase events around the world, scurry from pillar to post for want of a defense strategy worthy of the name. We have mistaken the army we must have between wars for the army that will deter or fight our next major war. The two are not remotely the same.

The Pentagon is unlikely to address—much less fix—these problems. We have "missioned" our forces by Pentagon turf battles rather than by strategic understanding. Senior military officers have been distanced from presidents and co-opted into a thickening national security bureaucracy. Their independent counsel has become muted at a time when their voice is much needed. Presidents and generals no longer make go-to-war decisions based on mutual respect and understanding.

The war in Iraq captured very little of the American way of war. The reason for going to war, to prevent the use of weapons of mass destruction against America or its allies, turned out to be unfounded and became just the first of a changing litany of causes offered to justify the action. We brought a strategy and an army sized and missioned for a short, force-on-force conflict when in fact the war we were starting was a long-term counterinsurgency. Senior officer dissent about this strategic miscalculation was stifled by the Pentagon civilian leadership and the White House. Our two wars against Iraq—Desert Storm in 1991 and the Iraq War beginning in 2003—yielded dramatically different results. Our army did not change; the wisdom and insight of our policymaking did.

The way ahead in defending America will be difficult. Where once defense of the nation was every citizen's responsibility, war has now become a government program, something that other people do for us. The values of our military remain intact but are challenged within an increasingly civilianized and politicized Pentagon. The connection between America and America going to war has become tenuous. The connection between America going to war and defending American freedom has become gossamer thin.

There are solutions to the challenges we face. We must understand America's role in the world and field a precision military force to support that role. We must reform the Pentagon, rethink our defense funding, and craft a sensible defense strategy. We must reconnect the American military and the American people, the core source of our strength, and then rebalance our military between standing forces and citizen soldiers. We must demand more from our leaders. And we must go to war only to defend America's freedom.

If we are to succeed, we must rise above political posturing and Pentagon tugs of war. The crisis we now face will not be resolved in the Pentagon or even in Washington. We are off course because the American public left these critical issues in the care of admirals, generals, and politicians. Defending America is not a line item in the federal budget. Our strength is the willingness of our people to defend their freedom: that rests squarely on the understanding and commitment of each American citizen.

There will be another major war in our future, despite the cottage industry of strategic thinkers who argue otherwise. They offer theories that wars between sovereign nations have been replaced by the friction of economic globalization, technology competition, or the mayhem of terrorism. That is wrong: history has not ended or even taken leave. And our past victories appear much more inevitable in hindsight than they did in the event. Our future victories and our ability to be a source of peace and stability in a troubled world are not at all assured. We are today more likely to lose our next war than we are to win it. And we do not know how long we have to get this right.

PART I
ADRIFT

CHAPTER 1:
The Warfight

IF YOU WANT TO UNDERSTAND the American way of war, a good place to begin is the bluff above the English Channel at Vierville on the coast of Normandy, France. That is where the Allied Army landed on June 6, 1944, to wrest Europe from Hitler's grasp. Go there in June in the early morning. It is something between chilly and cold in Normandy at that time of year, and the grass will still be wet from the night before.

As you look from the bluff toward the Channel, you are overlooking Omaha Beach, the scene of one of the critical battles of World War II.[1] This is difficult terrain to attack. You are standing on a hundred-foot bluff, a steep and forbidding barrier that runs the length of the beach. At low tide, the beach extends a hundred yards to the sea. To defend this place, the Germans planted a chain of steel barriers on the tidal flat, most with explosive mines, to stop landing craft from coming ashore. Several draws cut into the steep bluff, and in those draws the Germans built concrete gun emplacements. Machine gun positions and trenches lined the summit. German artillery and mortar positions inland had preplanned fires already registered on the beach.

As you stand on the high ground, it is easy to visualize the landing craft in the surf, infantrymen running across the flat sand beach at low tide. They fell, many of them, to the German fire. You can imagine the deep rumble of Allied fighters flying low overhead, headed inland looking for targets. You can envision the naval armada just offshore, waiting to land the second and third waves of soldiers and equipment.

Heavy and medium bombers began pounding the beach the morning of the invasion. Battleships, cruisers, and destroyers started a naval bombardment a half-hour before the first infantryman landed at 6:30 a.m. The generals and admirals thought the air and naval bombardments would kill or at the very least demoralize the German defenders in their concrete bunkers. Failing that, the massive air and naval fire support would pockmark the beach with holes from which the infantry soldiers could fire and maneuver. One minute before the first landing craft touched the beach, twenty rocket barges launched forty thousand rockets at the defenders. Tanks were outfitted with improvised flotation devices: they were to swim themselves ashore and lead the assault through the draws in the high bluff.

None of that worked. The aircraft missed the beach with their bombs. The naval gunfire was off target, by and large, because the beach was soon obscured by smoke and dust. The rockets landed everywhere but the beach. All but three of the thirty-two tanks launched floundered and sank coming ashore.[2] The three that made it to land were destroyed in short order. Some of the infantry landing craft were hit and sank before they reached the beach. Of those that did make it in, some boats had everyone—every soldier in the boat— killed before they could set foot ashore.

The first soldiers to land had to run through water and sand, weighted down with equipment and fatigued by hours afloat on a cold, turbulent sea. Despite the years of planning, despite the mass of weapons and equipment and firepower, despite the best efforts and courage of thousands of people, when the infantrymen got to the beach they were met with heavy German fire and a broad expanse of open, flat sand to run across.

Those that made it over the beach to the base of the bluff were wet, cold, disoriented, separated from their units, their leaders, and much of their equipment. These were not the squads, platoons, and companies that had trained for two years to fight this fight. By 8:30, there was so much carnage and wreckage at the water's edge that further landings were suspended. It is axiomatic in American military doctrine that a commander does not reinforce failure.

The American situation was desperate. The men ashore could not go forward. The plan to attack the draws with tanks had failed. They could not go back. There was no getting off the beach: the landing craft were full and circling offshore awaiting orders. They could not stay where they were. Mortar and artillery fire and the beach gun emplacements were taking a deadly toll.

What happened next says a lot about American soldiers. Leaders stepped forward: the occasional colonel, more captains and lieutenants, even more sergeants and privates. They blew holes in the barbed wire at the base of the bluff and crawled or ran through, taking one or two or three soldiers with them. It wasn't something anyone could order. It was something these soldiers just did. Many of the first ones through, perhaps most, were killed. Others kept coming, making their way up the slight depressions in the face of the bluff.

One of the two infantry regiments in the first wave ashore on Omaha Beach that morning was from the 29th Division of the Virginia National Guard. Bedford, a small town in central Virginia, lost nineteen people in the first hour of the invasion.[3] The line infantry divisions that fought from Normandy to the end of the war in Europe have been described as being three divisions: one in the cemetery, one in the hospital and one still fighting.

From the Channel, the plight of the soldiers ashore was obvious. Destroyer captains brought their ships perilously close to shore and gave the small groups of infantry direct fire support with their 5-inch guns. This wasn't planned, there was no elaborate coordination. They just did it.

As the morning wore on, a few soldiers made it to the top of the bluff and attacked the German fortifications in the draws from above.

By midday, the German fire had been suppressed enough to allow landings to resume. Casualties were still high in the second and third waves, but the American soldiers had taken the fight to the Germans and tipped the balance. Engineers blew the barriers in the draws and let the main attack force get off the beach.

There the day ended. The Allies were not far inland, not nearly as far as their plan called for. But they were ashore with room to continue landing forces. Almost everything that could go wrong with the American plan had gone wrong. Only the individual leadership, courage, and initiative of our soldiers won the battle.[4]

As you stand on the bluff at Omaha Beach, you can easily imagine the battle that was fought there. But that is not the place to end your visit. Turn and walk inland. In a few steps, you are in the American cemetery at Normandy. It is American soil, ceded by a grateful France in tribute to the valor of the Americans who liberated their country. The grounds are meticulously maintained, the trees and plants manicured to perfection. An overwhelming sense of order comes from the rows and rows of headstones, starkly aligned left and right, stretching into the distance. There are more than six thousand of them, each for an American who came so far from home and gave so much so that other people could be free. America had no designs on European territory, and certainly these individual Americans had no thoughts of gain. They were there to defend freedom—their own and Europe's. They did that well and at great cost.

We have a military to fight and win the nation's wars—what the people who do it every day call "the warfight"—but we are not able to do that now with any certainty. Today, we cannot fight battles like the one at Normandy, because we are adrift from the bedrock sources of our past victories.

After the implosion of the Soviet Union, the United States found itself by default the dominant conventional military power in the world. We'd been in a two-nation dead heat and the other nation dropped out of the race. To deal with that sudden change in fortune, the Pentagon cobbled together a post–Cold War military strategy. America was to shape the international environment to avoid war, maintain a military that could respond across the full spectrum of conflict, and prepare for future wars by buying the modern weapons systems that would assure battlefield dominance. The Pentagon shorthand description of that strategy was shape, respond, and prepare.

The first part of that strategy—shaping the international environment through American military presence around the world to deter conflicts and contain small wars—made sense then and makes sense now, but it proved to be a more challenging and consuming mission than the Pentagon envisioned. Collectively, these preventative measures are known as "engagement." The dimensions of our engagement workload became apparent as the United States sent troops to the Balkans in the mid-1990s.

The Balkans unraveled one town at a time. During the Balkan deployment, I was set to fly to a town on the Bosnia/Croatian border called Slavonski Brod. My helicopter broke. While the headquarters staff was looking for a replacement aircraft, I borrowed a Humvee and a couple of soldiers and took off overland. Going by ground is always a better way to get a sense of what is really going on.

The killing at Slavonski Brod started the night someone blew up the bridge across the Sava River in 1995. More Serbs than Croats and Muslims lived on the south side of the river, more Croats than Serbs on the north. That night, on the southern side of the river, the Serbs rounded up the Muslims who lived there, people who had been their neighbors and fellow townsmen for generations. The men were taken to the river's edge and shot, their bodies fell or were thrown into the broad Sava and floated downstream. The women and children became refugees, joining the thousands and then tens of thousands flooding the roads to escape the terror.

Across Bosnia, what would come to be described as "ethnic cleansing" spread. Long-standing religious, ethnic, and cultural hatreds that had been cosmetically salved during the Cold War erupted violently. Serbs against Croats against Bosnians, Christians against Muslims. The internecine bloodbath spread, people were taken into open fields and killed. Bosnia became a war with tanks and heavy weapons aimed largely at civilians. More than 250,000 would die before it was over. Sarajevo, which a few years before had genteelly hosted the Olympic games, came under military siege. Artillery shells rained down. People lived in cellars, there were shortages of power and water and food. Snipers in and around the city made sport of shooting scurrying civilians.[5] The siege of Sarajevo lasted forty-three months, the longest such battle since Stalingrad in World War II. To this day, many women in Sarajevo carry with them pictures of the children and loved ones they lost.[6]

As in World War I, the Balkan combatants each came to the conflict with big power sponsors. Russia supported the Serbs, the Islamic world the Muslims, Orthodox Christian groups their co-religionists. America and NATO wanted to avoid a wider war. The same ethnic and religious groups that were killing each other with such abandon in Bosnia were present in unstable proportions in the surrounding countries of Macedonia, Albania, Montenegro, and Slovenia. The potential for a wider European war was very real.

A series of UN resolutions, economic sanctions, and dire diplomatic warnings had limited impact. European countries sent military observers under UN sponsorship. They observed but did little more. In May 1995, the Serbs handcuffed UN observers to likely air targets to dissuade the use of American air power.[7]

After a gruesome massacre of Muslims by the Bosnian Serbs at Srebrenica, the United States bombed Serbian military positions and all sides came to a negotiating table at an air force base near Dayton, Ohio, an unlikely venue picked by the United States to isolate the negotiations and the negotiators. At American insistence, a fragile peace accord was signed by the leaders of Bosnia, Serbia, and Croatia. To implement that accord, the United States sent the 1st Armored Division as its part of the peacekeeping effort. They came into Bosnia in overwhelming force with tanks and infantry fighting vehicles, weapons loaded. For all intents and purposes, the United States and its NATO partners occupied Bosnia.

The killing stopped. The spread of unrest throughout this volatile region was staunched. Going in, we were worried that this would be another Vietnam, another interminable war fed by American casualties. That did not happen. Peace was not assured, but war was averted. The peacekeeping effort in Bosnia became a long-term commitment. Such deployments add to our defense budgets and wear out our people and our equipment. But the Bosnia peacekeeping mission, and the Kosovo deployment that followed, were much less troublesome and expensive than the war they prevented.

Today, around the world our forces engage in training exercises, humanitarian missions, peacekeeping operations, and counter-terrorist efforts. In any given year, the United States has forces in well over a hundred countries. These interwar tasks are worth doing. When done well, they prevent wars, but they also demand people, time, equipment, and money. What we failed to appreciate as the Cold War ended was that the interwar missions that America would face would stretch as far as the eye could see. We did not take into account the debilitating impact that our escalating interwar workload would have on our ability to fight conventional wars, that is, armed conflicts between the military forces of opposing nations.

America's conventional warfight is incredibly complex. How complex can be seen in a slice of a battle from the perspective of the command group of an infantry battalion as it goes to war. The commander is a lieutenant colonel, about forty years old and is the product of twenty years of intense career competition. He was among the best lieutenants, the best captains, the best majors. This colonel graduated near the top of every course of instruction the army put him through . . . and there were a lot of courses. He has succeeded at command and staff positions and is seen as having the potential to advance far in the army.

The commander and his staff have trained the battalion's three companies of combined infantry and tank platoons to a fine edge. They have a plan for the attack they are preparing to launch. They have staffed that plan, drawn it out on maps, rehearsed it on the ground, and fed it into computers. Their attack is part of a brigade plan, which is a part of the division and corps plans, and has been coordinated in detail with air force close air support and with the fire and maneuver plans of the units on their left and right flanks.

The battalion commander has battlefield operating systems that he must master: maneuver, command and control, mobility and counter-mobility, fire support, intelligence, and logistics.

The maneuver is what you see. That is precisely where the companies in the battalion go and precisely when they get there. Getting to a phase line several minutes early can put troops under friendly air bombardment or artillery fire. Getting there late can miss the tactical opportunity they came for in the first place.

Command and control is who gets to tell who what to do, phase lines and boundaries on a map, and who has first call on fires and routes and resupply.

Mobility is defeating the enemy's obstacles and barriers; counter-mobility is delaying and channeling the enemy's movement. Communications is the flow of information up and down the chain of command. That turns into several radio frequencies crowding the commander's squawk box in his armored personnel carrier, all the voices talking at the same time and all with some urgency.

Fire support means helicopter gunships, tactical air support, missiles, and artillery. Planning and timing supporting fires before they are needed is a big part of the battalion's plan.

Intelligence at this level is a reconnaissance plan, getting the scouts out, so they can flush out the enemy and screen the battalion's position. But the entire battalion, from the command group to each individual tank and infantry fighting vehicle, keeps track of tactical data from satellite and airborne sensors. Electronic icons show the location of every friendly and enemy vehicle on the battlefield, every aircraft in the air space over the battlefield, and a series of weather and chemical and control point graphic displays. It is a lot to look after.

The tanks in the battalion consume two gallons of fuel per mile; they will have to be refueled. Tank ammunition goes quickly; it will have to be replaced. Something on every tank will break almost every day; it will have to be fixed. Logistics is a once or twice a day event for this battalion and an all-day every day concern for the battalion commander.

The soldiers in the battalion trained for six months to a year in their individual job skills and then began squad, platoon, and company training. It takes several years to season sergeants to lead their squads, as long or longer to develop the junior officers to lead the platoons and companies. The army is fond of saying that it trains soldiers and grows leaders. That growth takes time, effort, and an unshakable commitment to high standards.

When the battalion goes to war, it represents years of recruiting and training efforts, more years of equipment and personnel decisions, and tens of millions of dollars of budget decisions. We can be the best in the world at this kind of battle and best by a significant margin. Our current conventional warfight is a decisive American advantage, but it requires time, training, and resources if it is going to work.

Our soldiers are not getting the time, training, or resources they need. The unending series of post–Cold War engagement missions has cut deeply into our conventional warfighting ability. If we send a battalion to a peacekeeping mission like the ones in Bosnia and

Kosovo, or a counterinsurgency tour in Iraq or Afghanistan, the conventional warfighting skills gained at such effort and expense fade quickly. A battalion bound for a peacekeeping mission or a counterinsurgency tour will train for a set of tasks—tasks that are very different than the warfight—for six months, go do those different things for a year or more, and then clean up and refit for six months after they get back. That process will prepare them to start the yearlong training for their conventional war mission. If they are scheduled for another overseas deployment, as many are, their chance to train for the warfight often gets lost in the shuffle. When they finally do get back to training for conventional war at the National Training Center (NTC) in the California desert, which is considered the capstone of our war training, almost every soldier and leader will have been assigned to the battalion since the last NTC rotation. They start from scratch.

The result is obvious. Engagement and counterinsurgency and counter-terrorism missions have cut deeply into our ability to fight conventional wars. While our forces are doing their interwar missions or fighting a counterinsurgency, they cannot maintain their conventional warfighting skills at the level required. Commanders, staffs, and soldiers gain skills and experience in any deployment: a combat-tested army is a better army. But engagement or counterinsurgency and conventional warfighting are different missions, and they require different training, different equipment, and different skill sets.

Even our best people can't be in two places at once. The army that we rely on as the core of our conventional warfight force is already deployed doing something else.

Our interwar workload and the preemptive war in Iraq have overdrawn our accounts in money, equipment, and people.

President Carter underfunded the Pentagon in the 1970s. When Ronald Reagan came to office, he tried to catch up by spending money by the handful. The air force got new aircraft, the army got tanks and infantry fighting vehicles, the navy new ships and submarines and carrier-based aircraft. After the Cold War ended, the funds budgeted for research and development and equipment procurement were diverted to pay the short-term fuel, payroll, and spare parts bills that came with America's ever expanding engagement strategy. The Iraq War brought with it a substantial increase in Pentagon funding, but that increase was more than offset by the cost of the war.

Quietly deferring research and procurement requirements to the budget's future years became the solution of choice. Every year, the Pentagon came up with PowerPoint slides showing an influx of research and procurement funding set to arrive in three to five years. And the next year's slides would show the same influx moved a year into the future. We never got there. If this was a family budget, we were buying food and paying the utility bills but not paying the mortgage and hoping that no one noticed. Capital spending short-falls, like missed mortgage payments, are cumulative. They do not go away just because they are not paid.

There is a downward spiral at work here. Older equipment breaks down more often and takes more time and money to keep operating. Helicopters that took twenty maintenance hours for each flight hour a few years ago now take over thirty. Tank engines that we planned to last 1,500 hours now last just 400. Vehicles that were budgeted and maintained to run 800 miles a year are being used 11,000 miles a year, and tanks projected to run 800 miles a year are running 4,000. The projected part of all this is more important than it at first appears because we buy parts, recruit and train mechanics, and build mainte-nance facilities based on projected use. Our forces are cannibalizing aircraft and ground vehicles, taking the parts off some to keep others flying and rolling. The ones left on blocks are called hangar queens, and the roster of hangar queens is growing.

Fixing this problem will take time. It takes at least eight to ten years to field a weapons system, closer to fifteen years for major systems. We keep those systems for a long time. Aircraft carriers will be in the fleet for forty years. Trucks will be on the ground for fifty years. Incredibly, some airplanes have been in the air for forty-five years and are expected to keep flying on for another thirty.[8] That is not just the same type of airplane, that is the same airframe. The systems that we are not replacing are wearing out.

The Pentagon checking account will stay overdrawn for the foreseeable future. The pay-right-now deployment bills keep coming in. Operating costs for older equipment keep rising. The recruiting incentives and pay levels required to attract and retain the high-quality volunteer force we have chosen are expensive. Some soldiers in critical skill areas can receive a reenlistment bonus of $150,000.[9] The Iraq War has proven costly: in constant-value dollars, we have spent many times as much money on regime change in Iraq as we spent on the entire Marshall Plan for all of Europe after World War II. However bleak our budget picture is, we must find a solution. Our engagement and warfighting strategies rest on high-quality recruits and technologically advanced equipment. A capital-based force requires capital, and we are not recapitalizing ours.

Our personnel account is overdrawn as well: our people are tired. "Unaccompanied tours" means that a soldier is based somewhere that his family can't be and we are now, more often than not, a married force. Overseas deployments, always unaccompanied, mean austere living conditions, long days, and the risk or reality of getting shot at. Unaccompanied tours and overseas deployments have become the rule now rather than the exception. We have something very much like a draft, but it only applies to those who have already served: under a policy the Pentagon calls "stop loss," we mandate that some people must stay in uniform even though their term of service is complete.

Our people in uniform are paying a high cost for these Washington misjudgments. One of the ground rules for planning military operations is not to rely on the courage of our soldiers to redeem a poorly planned mission.[10] Similarly, we should not rely on the dedication of our soldiers, sailors, airmen, and marines—and their families—to redeem poor policymaking in Washington.

Our combat readiness to fight a conventional war is in free fall. During the Cold War, our forces had one overarching mission: be prepared to fight the Soviet military forces as they came across the border of what was formerly called West Germany. So we focused our recruiting, equipping, training, and doctrine on that single task. We had forty years to plan and practice it all and, on active duty, the Pentagon fielded a combat-ready air force, army, navy, and marines. Vietnam gutted that force but we rebuilt. When Desert Storm came along, we had combat-ready units to send to war. They did the good job you would expect a rested and resourced force to do.

Today, we have an army that is not rested, not resourced and that dips well below combat-readiness in important areas. The wear and tear on people and equipment and the loss of training time that go with an unchecked appetite for engagement missions and long counterinsurgencies in Iraq and Afghanistan have severely limited our ground force ability to fight a conventional war.

Like the army, the other service branches rate themselves on readiness but there are different dynamics at work. As a rule, it is a bad idea to fly an airplane or an aircrew that is at less than peak readiness. In the last few years, the number of units in the air force that can hold that peak level has declined. Our airplanes are, on average, twenty-plus years old and headed for thirty-plus years old before any fixes will arrive. We need to be buying 170 airplanes a year to keep the air force fleet at a stable age. We are buying fewer than 100 a year.

The navy has yet another readiness equation. During the Cold War, the United States built toward and got close to a six-hundred-ship fleet. We now have something less than a three-hundred-ship navy, but the total number of days at sea for the fleet remains high. The results are predictable: a tiring fleet and strains on both equipment and people. We need to be building eight ships a year to maintain the current fleet: we are building half that number.[11]

The heart of the navy is the carrier battle groups. There are twelve of them, and the goal is to keep four at sea and on station at any given time. That number is driven as much from sheer mechanical availability as by any thoughtful global strategy. It takes six months to get a carrier battle group ready for a six-month deployment and six months to refit when it gets home. Only deployed carriers and their flying squadrons need to be at full-combat capability. So when they come back to port, the carrier battle groups purposely drop quickly to a rest and refit status. They stay at that lower readiness level until they deploy again. If you graph that readiness pattern over time, it looks like a bathtub. The problem is that the bathtub is getting deeper and the sides are getting steeper: the carriers are dropping more quickly after a deployment and not building back up until just before they sail. There have been times when the navy had to cross-deck people, parts, and airplanes. That rather innocuous sounding phrase of "cross-decking" means flying people and equipment from the carrier coming into port to the carrier leaving port. That extracts a heavy toll on the people and gear involved.

Occasionally the Pentagon gets too clever. When the navy was trying to expand the fleet to six hundred ships, they dispersed carrier battle groups to ports that—not coincidentally—had strong Congressional delegations. When the navy had to downsize the fleet, they had to wrestle with Congress to have fewer carrier battle groups: that long-cultivated support became resistance.

The "emperor is naked" factor that usually goes unnoticed outside the Pentagon—it is perhaps one level too arcane—is that America's military is an expeditionary force. We are not going to war with either Mexico or Canada. The United States fields forces equipped and trained to deploy and fight in some far distant country. For more than a hundred years, America's role as a world power has required expeditionary forces that can deploy around the world. Few other nations even attempt to do so and no other nation does it nearly as well.

It takes ships and planes to move and sustain those forces. During the Cold War, we had many of our units permanently stationed overseas, near where they would fight. They could drive to work. After the Cold War, we shrank our entire force by something more than a third and our overseas force by as much as two-thirds. Most of our forces are now based in the continental United States. That means we have to transport those forces to where their mission will be. We put people and high-priority equipment on planes and the vast majority of our equipment, up to 90 percent of it, on ships. Those ships and planes are our airlift and sealift assets.

America's lift capability translates into a very precise number. That number is the tally of weight and cubic volume and days at sea or flying hours from point A to point B. Big computers crunching reams of data. Deep thinkers may wax eloquent all they like about grand strategies but the starting point for America's military capabilities is a very hard data point: how much we can move how far and how long it will take.

Our military capabilities must pass through this narrow portal of lift. The Pentagon leadership can add and subtract and they know they have to widen the portal. Perhaps more ships and planes, perhaps more pre-positioned equipment overseas, perhaps lighter equipment and less of it, perhaps more lethal but smaller forces. More likely, a combination of all of these measures and more.

Our lift fixes are still multi-year fixes if we started today, and we are not starting today. So, for the foreseeable future, we will have to plan our engagement and warfight workload with the lift we have now. We can move everything we have to move, but it will take longer than we want. That is why the Desert Storm build-up took six months, the Iraq War build-up, with a force less than a third the size of Desert

Storm, five months. During the Cold War, we could field ten divisions in Europe in ten days. Today, we can field six divisions to the theaters where war is likely in six months.

Major wars have determined our nation's fate in the past and they will do so in the future. All of America's major wars came as surprises: our next major war will as well. Our warfight capability is not now what it needs to be to deal with that surprise. We have stretched and stressed our forces in an unending series of between-war missions and an elective war in Iraq and we have diverted the time and resources needed to maintain our conventional war capability. We are not recapitalizing our force. Our people and equipment are tired. We have changed from a forward deployed force to a power projection force and have yet to solve the serious lift limitations that resulted.

America spends heavily on defense. We have committed and capable men and women in our ranks, but we are not ready to fight anything approaching a major war. Even worse, we are not confronting the issues that will allow us to do so.

CHAPTER 2:

The Pentagon

THE PROSPECT OF FIXING THE WARFIGHT by doing business the way the Pentagon now does business is remote. We routinely make bad decisions there because of how we make those decisions, too often behind an opaque screen of bureaucracy. We can remove that screen: the key players are identifiable enough to be held accountable. They are the military services, the theater combatant commanders, the secretary of defense, and the chairman of the Joint Chiefs of Staff.

The services—the army, navy, air force, and marines—are headquartered in the Pentagon. Each is headed by a four-star flag officer, a general for the army, the air force, and the marines and an admiral in the navy's case. The service senior staffs are also there, platoons of generals and battalions of colonels. All of the services have the same mission: to recruit, train, and equip warfighting forces. That is a big job but it is their only job. The services are not involved in fighting wars or running engagement, peacekeeping, or counter-terrorism operations abroad.

The warfighters are not in the Pentagon. They are the theater combatant commanders, also four-star generals and admirals, who have headquarters of their own, usually located in the theater for which they are responsible. It is the combatant commanders who plan for and fight conflicts like Desert Storm and the Iraq War. They also plan and conduct overseas deployments like the smaller-scale contingencies in Haiti, Bosnia, and Kosovo. The combatant commanders direct the forces provided by the services. The two missions—recruit, train, and equip by the services and warfighting by the combatant commanders—are largely separate missions. And they should be; both are full-time jobs.

In Desert Storm, for example, each service sent the land, sea, or air forces called for in the central command theater commander's war plan. The services had been getting ready to do just that for years, in fact: size themselves, buy equipment, and train specifically to execute our war plans. So when the United States decided to go to war to contest Saddam Hussein's invasion of Kuwait, the theater commander in Southwest Asia did not have to worry about whether his forces would show up trained, whether they would have the right equipment, or whether they would arrive more or less on time. That was and is the services' job. General Norman Schwarzkopf could use his time and talents and his thousand-person headquarters revising his basic war plan, fine-tuning a campaign plan, getting his logistics systems up and running, marshaling and maneuvering his forces, working with Coalition allies, fighting the war, and dealing with political oversight and suggestions from Washington.

The service/combatant commander division of labor works and is largely free of the debilitating turf battles that plague the Pentagon: officers flow back and forth between the two camps and the weight of the mission keeps our uniformed officers focused. But four-stars being four-stars, this sometimes gets a bit prickly. The service chiefs occasionally offer unsolicited suggestions to the theater commanders about warfighting and the combatant commanders occasionally toss barbs at the services but, almost all the time, collegiality prevails. The breakdowns in Pentagon decision making most often occur between civilians and our senior military officers, both in the services and in the combatant commands. Those civilians are headed by the secretary of defense.

When Congress established the position of secretary of defense in 1947, it wasn't the secretary of defense we now know and it wasn't called that. The title in the legislation was secretary of the National Military Establishment, a description that more accurately reflected the job then as the titular head of the still independent military services.[1] The civilian secretaries of those services were then members of the president's cabinet. The secretary of the Military Establishment was not and so had little real authority. This rather strained Congressional compromise emerged from the bitter debates over service unification that followed World War II. General Marshall, General Eisenhower, and President Truman all pressed hard for more unification, what we would now call joint operations. The service lobbies in Congress, principally the navy's, opposed it. Hence the National Military Establishment minuet.

Several times since 1947, Congress has legislatively moved away from service autonomy toward a more joint approach. In that process, the secretary of defense has gone from titular to very real. The secretary of defense is now in the chain of command between the president and his four-star combatant commanders and is a member of both the president's cabinet and the National Security Council. The service secretaries are none of those things. Being in the chain of command, in particular, has a specific meaning to generals and admirals: you are supposed to do what the commander says. Secretaries of defense have that level of statutory authority.

Civilians are in charge in the Pentagon. Whether they do that well or poorly, they are still in charge. Civilians set policy and then expect uniformed officers to run the military in accord with the policies set by the secretary of defense and his legion of civilian staffers. That theory usually comes up short. The uniformed services will enthusiastically follow any civilian policy decision that advances the cause of their service and will drag their feet on any policy decision that does not. Stonewalling by a service can easily consume a decade and can withstand a great deal of civilian prodding. The tilt-rotor V-22 aircraft has been in procurement and testing—unsuccessfully to date—for thirty years, despite many efforts to write it off as a bad idea. For a secretary of defense to kill a service-favored program is a rare and wrenching event.

Civilians also have an ongoing tug of war with the combatant commanders. Secretaries of defense sign orders authorizing overseas deployments. That authority allows a take-charge secretary to set the size and type of force that goes to war or deploys for an engagement mission. Generals will usually have a different force in mind, often a significantly different force. As a practical matter, convoluted negotiations between uniformed officers and the secretary's civilian staff produce a committee-designed force deploying to execute a committee-written plan.[2]

One part of the Pentagon that does work is the position of chairman of the Joint Chiefs of Staff. Chairmen are normally queued up by secretaries of defense, personally selected by presidents, and confirmed by the Senate. The chairman is, by law, the senior officer in the American military. That statute has little impact. Chairmen command no forces and are not in the chain of command. Their authority comes from our traditions and our history.

Americans have long harbored a wariness of super grade military officers. Since the first general staff was formed at the War Department in 1903, there have been statutory limits on the size and scope of any general staff organization in Washington.[3] There are lingering remnants of those limitations today and they do little harm. The chairman's primary responsibility is to be the principal military adviser to the president and the secretary of defense. That may not sound like a powerhouse role but in reality it is.

The central issue at work here is the thoroughly ingrained idea of civilian control of the military. That fact lies so deeply within our officer corps that it properly goes unconsidered. Because the chairman has been the conduit of that civilian authority, the primary interface between civilian and military leadership, his opinion has been the final word within uniformed military councils. The other four-stars call the chairman "sir." Prior to the Iraq War, challenges to the chairman's lone status as the interface with civilian authority, even challenges that were statutorily sanctioned, were both infrequent and unwelcome.[4] If our chairmen had outright command of all U.S. forces, their actual authority would be hardly greater than it already is today and their critical role as counselors to presidents would fade to nothing.

Chairmen have earned their authority. After World War II, Dwight Eisenhower served briefly in a chairman-like role. Omar Bradley was the first official chairman. He and the other early chairmen were limited by the fact that advice to the president was at that time a committee function held by the entire Joint Chiefs of Staff, a relic of the service unification battles following World War II. Forthright counsel was often lost in a deluge of color-coded paperwork for concurrences, non-concurrences, and minority positions. Pointed advice to presidents was rare. After the Goldwater-Nichols reform legislation of 1986 invested responsibility for advising the president principally in the chairman, the office and those in it came into their own.

It does civilians well to remember that the source of a chairman's power is his role as the conduit between civilian leadership and people in uniform. How chairmen are valued and used by presidents and secretaries of defense determines how effective they can be. Increased authority for secretaries of defense should not mean decreased authority for senior military officers. Robert McNamara made that mistake for the Vietnam War, Donald Rumsfeld for the Iraq War. McNamara enforced businesslike processes and metrics to manage combat power in a war that could not be won with combat power. Rumsfeld accomplished what he thought was his mission— defeat the Iraqi Army in battle—but he had fundamentally misread the mission. Senior military officers should have been able to correct these missteps had they been at the center of final defense decisions.

The current Pentagon way of doing business has separated presidents from their senior military officers. Presidents and generals as a rule no longer understand one another, no longer work in concert, no longer come to be of one mind about war policy. Our slide from the Roosevelt/Marshall model—which worked well in World War II—has been clear and consistent.

When Franklin Roosevelt involved himself in the details of military decision making, he usually got it wrong. In the tense years before Pearl Harbor, Roosevelt airily called for an increase in aircraft production to the unheard of level of ten thousand planes a year. What seemed to elude him was that planes produced without the trained crews to man them, the mechanics to maintain them, and the bases and hangers to house them were of little value. Roosevelt heard that bit of troubling news from a brigadier general newly arrived in town, a general unschooled enough in the Washington way of things to blurt out his disagreement with the president in a room full of senior policymakers. The others in the room thought Roosevelt would end George Marshall's career then and there. They underestimated both men.[5]

In the highly successful Roosevelt/Marshall way of doing business, Roosevelt had a gift for fashioning a sound strategic framework and then left the operational issues in Marshall's care. Within Roosevelt's guidance, Marshall had wide latitude. In late 1942, on the eve of Congressional elections, there was considerable pressure to get American troops into the war somewhere. The landings in North Africa were imminent, but selecting the actual day of the invasion rested with Marshall and Dwight Eisenhower, the field commander. They looked at tide tables and daylight data and ships available and steaming time—everything except the politics of the event. The invasion took place four days after the election.[6] That level of priority for operational issues at the expense of political concerns is unthinkable in the current Washington environment.

President Truman resisted the growing national security bureaucracy. He viewed the congressionally mandated National Security Council as an infringement on his presidential power and seldom convened NSC meetings. Truman's buck-stops-here decisiveness, coupled with his high regard for the generals and admirals who fought and won World War II, continued the civil/military success that Roosevelt and Marshall achieved, even to the extent of dealing with the Korean War insubordination of Douglas MacArthur.

Eisenhower had an enormous advantage as president in dealing with defense matters. He was in the White House because of his stature as a soldier. He also knew more about warfighting than the generals and admirals then serving in the Pentagon. From that secure pinnacle, Eisenhower used the National Security Council as staff support for his own decision making, a process very similar to his experience as a general. The surprise, perhaps, is the priority that Eisenhower gave civilian concerns. He understood that one of the foundations of America's military strength is its civilian economy. Given a choice between the health of the civilian economy and additional military expenditures, Eisenhower chose the economy almost every time and that was the right choice: Eisenhower's foresight on the power of a strong economy ultimately proved to be one of the principal sources of America's Cold War success. His foresight on how not to address defense issues was equally astute: his parting admonition to be concerned about the influence of a military-industrial complex cautioned us not to make decisions the way we now make decisions.

John Kennedy was dramatically less successful than Eisenhower as commander in chief. Neither he nor his secretary of defense placed great value in the counsel of the Joint Chiefs of Staff.[7] Civilian staffers in the White House and at the Pentagon became increasingly important, while senior military officers became increasingly distanced from final defense decision making.

The White House/Pentagon process was broken by the time Lyndon Johnson faced a go-to-war decision in Vietnam in 1965. As the deployment of American combat forces to Vietnam grew, the Joint Chiefs of Staff asked to exercise their statutory right to consult directly with the president. That request was not a routine event. The senior officers charged with responsibility for America's military were challenging the authority of an aggressive secretary of defense, Robert McNamara, something he never took lightly.

The Chiefs got their meeting, without McNamara present. When the chairman and the service chiefs entered the oval office, President Johnson did not offer them seats. Standing around a map of Vietnam being held by a nervous marine major, the senior officers of each of our military services made a case for a military response with military missions against North Vietnam. This was very different than the McNamara approach of a gradual application of combat power to signal political intent. Gradualism was a policy favored by the civilians in the Pentagon, the State Department, and the White House staff.[8] However, the Joint Chiefs did not view land battles and B-52 air strikes as signaling devices.

Johnson listened for a few minutes and then began to berate his generals in profane and personally insulting language. After a long, loud and demeaning tirade, the president called them idiots and told them to "get the hell out of my office."[9] That such a scene could have taken place indicates a disastrously poor state of civil/military relations.

As too often happens, the Washington bureaucracy developed a policy to meet the perceived desires of a president. Johnson's senior advisers told him what he wanted to hear about Vietnam and what they told him was wrong. Graduated pressure had worked during the Cuban missile crisis, McNamara's formative policymaking experience. He and his lawyerlike inner circle assumed that the North Vietnamese would act like the "reasonably prudent man" that underlies Western common law tradition.[10] But the North Vietnamese were fighting what they believed was a war of national liberation, not an endeavor that lends itself to either reasonableness or prudence. They had defeated one Western power in battle—France—and had little compunction about fighting another.

McNamara also favored a comfortably businesslike approach to the war in Vietnam: input and output, numbers and graphs. What had worked for McNamara at Ford Motor Company did not work for America in Vietnam. McNamara and his minions mistook activity for progress. The body counts tallied and tons of bombs dropped were charted as successes. The real utility of McNamara's policy of gradualism was to allow Johnson to downplay his government's growing commitment to a war in Vietnam.

Politics played too great a role in Vietnam policymaking. Rather than make a go-to-war decision on the merits, both Kennedy and Johnson focused on the domestic political impact of their Vietnam decisions. President Kennedy appears to have decided to withdraw from Vietnam but delayed taking that step until after the 1964 presidential elections, lest he appear appeasingly soft on Communism. His assassination in late 1963 ended any chance of that planned withdrawal. Upon assuming the presidency, President Johnson decided to escalate the American commitment in Vietnam but delayed that step until after the 1964 presidential elections, lest he appear too much the warmonger. Both presidents let their reelection needs drive their Vietnam policymaking.[11]

Presidents set the level and tone of the military counsel they receive. Success requires a meeting of the minds between presidents and their senior military officers. John Kennedy and Lyndon Johnson never achieved that level and kind of communication.

Civilian decision making for military operations has now become painfully detailed. The White House staff gives approval of specific tactical bombing targets. The White House press office sends teams to coach combat commanders before major press conferences to keep their generals on message. Secretaries of defense try to insert their civilian staffers in the war planning process conducted by the theater commanders.[12] Meetings between presidents and senior military officers have become largely ceremonial, affixing the presidential imprimatur to civilian-developed decisions and allowing presidents to assert that they consulted their generals.

The Pentagon currently produces war plans that are more fiction than fact. They are based on being able to fight a Desert Storm–size conflict either in Korea or Southwest Asia while being prepared to fight a second one of the same size somewhere else.[13] Our engagement and contingency operations and counter-terrorism efforts, the Haitis and Bosnias and Kosovos of the world, take up at least another Desert Storm–size commitment of land, sea, and air forces. Deadly but only moderately sized conflicts in Iraq and Afghanistan emptied the tanks of our army and, for a time, ruled out any other large military commitments anywhere for any purpose.

The force we had for Desert Storm was the on-the-shelf remnant of our large Cold War force. Then we had sixteen army divisions on active duty. Today we have ten. For Desert Storm, we drew from an air force of thirty-six fighter wing equivalents. Today we have twenty. The Desert Storm navy had fifteen carrier battle groups and a total fleet of over five hundred ships. Today we have twelve carrier battle groups, headed to eleven, and a fleet of fewer than three hundred ships.

Our war plans are unrealistically optimistic, in part because we have missioned our forces and planned our future by Pentagon turf battles rather than by strategic understanding. From the end of the American Revolution until the Cold War, the role of the regular military was to perform interwar missions. That regular force role had been garrisoning an expanding frontier, exercising gunboat diplomacy, and preventing war. There was no thought that regular forces would fight our wars, they would be the core around which large citizen soldier forces were raised when war came. That is how our Constitution envisioned defending America and how our previous victories were achieved.

We misplaced that wisdom in the four decades of the Cold War. Our strategy then required a big army based in Europe to deter an invasion by the Soviet Union. That was the right strategy to meet that threat, but the sudden demise of the Soviet Union made forty years of war plans and preparations almost completely irrelevant.

As a carryover from our Cold War success, we still assume that our standing military will fight our wars. That won't work. Since the Cold War ended, we have put too many missions—warfighting, engagement, peacekeeping, counter-terrorism, natural disaster response, equipment and doctrine experimentation, and homeland defense—on our active duty force. When the Berlin Wall came down, the Pentagon thought it could meet the post–Cold War emerging missions with a dramatically reduced military and still keep that same force as our conventional war force. We called the new interwar missions "lesser included tasks," meaning that a combatant unit could do them by virtue of its warfighting skills and still carry responsibility for the warfight. Military units can refocus to engagement and other missions and succeed, but America's escalating interwar workload has severely limited the ability of that same force to fight a conventional war.

The Pentagon got off course in missioning our forces because of how it makes these kinds of decisions. After the Cold War, it was clear that America would have to get by with a much smaller military. Civilian budget analysts enthusiastically began surgery on the Pentagon budget to find an always elusive peace dividend. Within the Pentagon, it became apparent that giving up old missions or not signing up for new missions meant giving up funding.

As could be expected, each part of the force said it could do each and every mission—the old ones, the new ones, and the ones that were just a gleam in someone's eye. Bureaucracies seldom opt for their own eclipse. Active duty generals get to frame these decisions for secretaries of defense, so our active duty forces remained our first line warfighters and became first to deploy constabulary force for engagement missions. They were also the experimentation force that would take and test new equipment and doctrine, a force for hurricane relief, and a force for homeland defense. All of those missions, all at the same time, all with the same priority inside the Pentagon: defend the army—or navy or air force or marine—turf. Budget-driven enthusiasm was substituted for strategic vision.

Part of what was and is going on here is that, given a choice between being a general of a warfighting force or of a peacekeeping force, generals will pick the warfight role every time. There has been a long-standing tension between the constabulary missions that the country needs between wars and the warfighting missions that generals and admirals fancy.

The Pentagon—hampered by bureaucratic battles between civilian and uniformed leaders and with senior officers bureaucratically distanced from presidents—is unlikely to resolve the fundamental issues required to renew America's military might. Our two wars against Iraq benchmark our policymaking drift.

CHAPTER 3:

Two Wars Against Iraq

AMERICAN VICTORIES ARE STILL ACHIEVABLE. Our two wars against Iraq show how wars can be won decisively and, regrettably, how they can sidestep into a strategic morass. Desert Storm in 1991 captured almost all of the fundamentals of our past success and was a clear victory. The Iraq War beginning in 2003 captured very little of the bedrock sources of our past success and became a costly misadventure. These very different results came not from a lessening of the battlefield capabilities of our military forces, which in fact increased significantly, but rather from flawed policymaking.

It is an open question whether the American intelligence community was caught flat-footed by Saddam Hussein's invasion of Kuwait in August 1990. The high priests of the occult art of intelligence all have different versions of what they knew and when they knew it.[1] That does not matter, really. The fact was that our military forces had to rush to war half a world away, the kind of deployment envisioned in our war plans then and now.

Saddam rolled his tanks and armored personnel carriers into Kuwait City just three hours after the invasion began, to the Saudi Arabian border in two days.[2] There was little armed opposition. The Iraqis halted at the all but undefended Saudi border for reasons known only to Saddam. Certainly not because there were any forces there that could have stopped him.

The first two American aircraft carriers were on station, ready to launch aircraft, in six days.[3] The first American ground combat forces, the lightly armed ready brigade of the 82nd Airborne Division, were in place a week after the invasion.[4] The 82nd could not have stopped Saddam's armored force: the paratroopers of the 82nd, in the wonderful way American soldiers have of telling the truth, called themselves speed bumps for Iraqi tanks. The first U.S. Air Force combat aircraft, ten squadrons of F-15 and F-16 fighters, arrived in Saudi Arabia within two weeks of the invasion. Each squadron brought 24 aircraft and 1,500 mechanics, armorers, and technicians.[5] The American military had the forces in place in Saudi Arabia to begin a counteroffensive to retake Kuwait within six months.[6]

The American deployment to the Persian Gulf for Desert Storm was impressive: half a million troops, thousands of vehicles, and many millions of tons of cargo. These were not just gaggles of people and piles of equipment. The American military goes to war in functionally defined units that must fit together. Each tank battalion that went to Desert Storm had fifty-four tanks in it, each with a crew of four. The infantry battalions had fifty-eight armored personnel carriers, each with a squad of eleven infantrymen. That was the ground warfighting force. But to bring that combat power to bear, a port-handling unit had to be in place to get the equipment on a ship in the United States and another set of port handlers had to be in Saudi Arabia to get it off the ship. Truck companies were in place in ports in Saudi Arabia to move the people and the equipment to staging areas. Maintenance companies deployed to keep all that heavy iron in motion. Spare parts and ammunition and fuel resupply systems were up and running. Medics, clerks, chaplains, cooks and a hundred other kinds of specialists were on hand. Eighty percent of our forces support the twenty percent that are maneuver combat units. They all have to be there and they all have to be working.

The hardest part of a Desert Storm–type deployment is the people. The tank crews and infantry squads must be trained on a wide range of demanding tasks. That training takes months. Their leaders have to be proficient at synchronizing complex fire and maneuver and communications and intelligence systems to see the battle, fight it and win it. That training takes years.

Now extend that movement, equipping, sustainment, and training requirement to artillery, aviation, and a dozen other branches of the army and then expand the task to include the air force, navy, and the marines. Deployments like Desert Storm are not just questions of size. The real challenge is to make the moving parts fit together.

One of the successes of Desert Storm was our use of the citizen soldiers in our reserve components. When Saddam Hussein invaded Kuwait, he knew nothing at all about Alpha Company, U.S. Marine Corps Reserve, stationed at Fort Knox, Kentucky.

Alpha Company contained 138 marines. They were all reservists who had full-time jobs as schoolteachers, bartenders, mechanics, and dozens of other callings. They trained on weekends and during the summer for about forty days a year. Their commander was a brand-new marine Reserve captain. The tanks assigned to Alpha Company were less than fearsome. They were M-60A1s, three or four generations behind the army's then current main battle tank. Based on 1950s technology, the A-1s had a 105mm main gun (considerably smaller than more modern tanks) outdated sights, and limited firing range. The U.S. government had taken more modern tanks and dropped them at sea to act as artificial reefs.

Alpha Company mobilized at Thanksgiving and was in the desert for New Year's Eve. They were assigned to 6th Marine Regiment, 2nd Marine Division. The company drew equipment in the desert, the same 1950s version M-60A1s they had trained on in Kentucky.

Alpha Company was to lead the marine assault in their sector to breach the Iraqi defensive line. That would be a tough mission. The Iraqis had two defensive belts in place, each a hundred yards or more in depth, separated by perhaps three-quarters of a mile of desert. Those defensive belts consisted of dense minefields, ditches and obstacles covered by tanks, direct fire anti-tank weapons and artillery. The Iraqi plan was to use its numerical advantage in artillery to destroy the American forces bogged down in the minefields. Alpha Company was thought likely to take high casualties, perhaps as high as 80 percent. If they made it through the assault intact, their orders were to dig in on the far side of the second defensive belt. The better-equipped follow-on marine units would pass through them and take over the attack.

It didn't happen exactly that way. On the morning the ground war started, Alpha Company moved out and crossed the Kuwait border at 5:05 a.m. Marine Corps engineers fired line charges into the first defensive belt. Those charges were essentially 1,800 pounds of sausage-shaped high explosives tied end to end and fired like a rope. When the engineers blew the line charges, they opened a narrow lane through the minefield. Alpha Company rolled through it and kept moving. When they got to the second defensive belt, they launched more line charges and found more good luck: the Iraqi artillery fire was poorly coordinated and kept falling behind them. That was hard on the units moving up behind them, but Alpha Company made it through the breach, losing only two tanks to land mines. By noon, they were rolling across the open desert, shooting, getting shot at, and moving further and faster than anyone expected.

The plan of attack was changed. Since Alpha Company was still combat effective and moving forward, they would continue to lead the assault. The company stopped that night and let the rest of the attacking force close up. At dawn on the second day, they moved out again. They were entering the battle space where they would face better-equipped Iraqi forces.

At midday, the wind shifted and heavy smoke from burning oil wells obscured their line of advance. Because the M-60A1s had no thermal sights, Alpha Company was all but blind. They called for their supporting artillery to fire illumination rounds, a parachute flare designed to light up the battlefield at night. The flares didn't work in the opaque smoke. The Alpha Company commander had his artillery reset the flares to land on the ground to his front to guide his advance. The company kept moving.

That afternoon, still blanketed in black smoke, the platoon sergeant of 3rd Platoon radioed to the company commander that there was a darker shape to his uniformly dark front.[7] Directed to fire on it, the platoon sergeant's first round hit a powerful Russian-built T-72 tank at four hundred yards. For tanks, that is extremely close. The burning tank illuminated a line of Iraqi T-72 and T-62 tanks. Alpha Company attacked and a running gun battle erupted. The marines kept coming. What began at four hundred yards ended at sixty yards, tank on tank with main guns. The Iraqi tanks were destroyed.

By the end of the third day, Alpha Company was on the outskirts of Kuwait City. Arab forces passed through their position to enter the Kuwaiti capital unopposed. That is where the cease-fire found Alpha Company the next day.[8]

In four days of combat, Alpha Company destroyed numerous enemy tanks, armored personnel carriers, and trucks, and it also captured three hundred Iraqi soldiers while suffering no casualties from enemy fire. They fought with equipment that was, by any standard, out of date. They were reserve marines, young, with no combat experience before Desert Storm, and few had spent much time on active duty. They succeeded because of the initiative of the young marines in the company, the leadership of their sergeants and officers, and the commitment of their senior leaders that they could and would perform their mission.

The Alpha companies in the marines, army, air force, and navy reserve components are now the first echelon of the citizen soldier armies that fought and won our major wars. But, in the turf-conscious Pentagon, the idea that citizen soldiers can be the nation's warfight force—as they have done for two centuries, for every successful war in our history—is viewed as dangerous heresy.

Much of the American way of war was intact for Desert Storm. The cause was arguably compelling: nations should not be allowed to invade other nations, because such unchecked aggression leads to wider wars. Strategic insight was brought to bear by both civilian and military leaders. The president set a clear mission—expel the invading Iraqi Army from Kuwait—and then made a case that won wide international support. The senior uniformed officers involved were given broad authority, and they developed and executed a winning campaign plan. The citizen soldiers of the Guard and Reserve were called up—the first such widespread use since the Korean War—helping make this war all of America's war. Congress was not asked to declare war, but a sharply debated Authorization for the Use of Military Force Against Iraq Resolution served something approaching the same purpose. Our values were intact. America's freedom was not directly attacked, but the menace to America was clear: Saddam Hussein as a Middle East hegemon would mean a wider war, and soon.

In Desert Storm, our victory was decisive. For the second Iraq War, the fundamentals of the American way of war were largely absent.

The cause for going to war against Iraq a second time was not only not compelling, it was neither clear nor consistent. It was first to prevent the use of weapons of mass destruction, then to help the Iraqi people, then to foster the spread of democracy in the Middle East, then to combat global terrorism. All good and worthy goals, but a cause for going to war should be self-evident. Compelling causes compel war. Elective wars like the Iraq War are matters of choice, not matters of the nation's survival.

In Desert Storm, the president and the secretary of defense chose to communicate with their warfighting theater commander through the chairman of the Joint Chiefs of Staff. That president and that secretary were not wilting violets but chose to use the chairman—Colin Powell—as their channel of communication to the warfighters and, whether they knew it or not, as a translator and gatekeeper of information moving in both directions.[9] The arrangement worked well. For Desert Storm, strategy and force size and mission issues surfaced and were successfully resolved both before and during the war.

For the Iraq War, the secretary of defense decided to deal directly with his theater commander, Tommy Franks, as he had the statutory right to do. The secretary rewrote the war plan to reflect how he thought the war should be fought. The initial plan of the senior generals and admirals at Central Command and the Pentagon was based on a robust force of 385,000.[10] The civilian leadership in the Pentagon, based on some optimistic assumptions that turned out not to be accurate, whittled that force down to 150,000. Once the war was underway, the secretary held video teleconferences with the ground commander in Iraq to get feedback and give direction.

For the Iraq War, our senior uniformed officers were co-opted into civilian decision making. Without independent and forceful counsel, the civilians in the Pentagon and the White House sent a force sized for and prepared to fight a short force-on-force war against a depleted Iraqi military. The war they were actually starting was a long-term counterinsurgency, the occupation of a deeply divided country to implement not just a régime change but a change in basic approaches to governance among fundamentally inimical regions, religions, and cultures. Cogent military counsel about the likelihood and costs of an extended occupation of Iraq did not make it into the final policy decisions for the war.

There was dissent among our senior officers at the time, and how that dissent was handled does not speak well for how the Pentagon and the White House now do business. The chief of staff of the army, Gen. Rick Shinseki, was skeptical of secretary Rumsfeld's downsizing of the force going to war. The secretary of defense announced the chief of staff's replacement fifteen months before his twenty-four-month term of service was to be completed, a not very subtle invitation for the general to resign. To his credit, Shinseki did not.[11] Responding to congressional questioning, he said that the force being sent could be too small and that the mission could well extend beyond the short combat phase into a long-term commitment.[12] Senior civilians at the Pentagon and in the White House described Shinseki's position as wildly off the mark.

The lack of strategic insight evident in how we began the second war in Iraq continued into the occupation. The Pentagon retained responsibility for the American effort there and was slow to understand the nature of the challenge it faced. For the first year of the insurgency, the senior civilian leadership at the Pentagon and in the White House resisted using the term "insurgency," lest it conjure up unhelpful comparisons to Vietnam. The in-country Coalition Provisional Authority, a hastily thrown together Pentagon effort headed by a civilian, thought it could reestablish a functioning Iraq better than could the Iraqis. They sought to remake Iraq in America's image. Iraqi elections, structured by the United States, required a quota of 25 percent female winners.[13] The CPA uprooted the previous government and disbanded the army, one of the few sources of stability in Iraq. In the ensuing turmoil, religious sectarian violence made the things that could win a counterinsurgency for the tenuous Iraqi government—a secure environment and a functioning economy—very difficult.

All of America did not go to war in Iraq. The Guard and Reserve were used, but the Reserve components had become an adjunct of the standing force: the rallying impact of their use was lessened. There was no rush of citizens to recruiting stations. For the Iraq War, maintaining even the normal levels of recruiting for our volunteer force proved painfully difficult. Standards were changed—arguably lowered—and enlistment bonuses were raised.

Our values became blurred. The Iraq War was more similar to the Vietnam conflict than our political leaders wanted to admit. Using the U.S. Army to establish and to keep in power a tenuous Iraqi government in the face of a deadly insurgency inescapably placed our forces in an ethical kill zone. Only a very small number of our soldiers forfeited their values, but the impact of that loss in a media-saturated war was widespread.

Prisoner abuse in Iraq and Afghanistan were symptoms that our leadership had failed. The White House staff authored memos that made torture as a policy less clearly repugnant and more permissible. Our civilian intelligence agencies kidnapped people in foreign countries and took them to secret prisons overseas, where their mistreatment was anticipated. Prison guards at Abu Ghraib and elsewhere were operating under interrogation rules personally revised by the secretary of defense thousands of miles away and multiple layers of command removed. A command climate that tolerated abuses was created.[14] The president resisted, in fact vetoed, statutory prohibitions against the use of torture. We forgot who we are.

A connection between going to war in Iraq and defending America's freedom was not obvious. The most consistently offered cause for the war came to be the need to battle global terrorism. Combating terrorism is not war. It is a critical threat that must be faced, but the Washington ploy of calling counter-terrorism a "war" is not helpful. On September 11, 2001, the U.S. Army owned something on the order of 7,900 Abrams tanks, the U.S. Air Force 3,100 war planes, and the U.S. Navy fleet contained 300 ships.[15] The terrorists owned none. If America had possessed twice the tanks, planes, and ships, it would have made no difference. Fighting terrorism is not about military power and certainly not about American military power.

Miscasting counter-terrorism as war was an understandable error. The events of September 11th were disorienting. The American homeland was under attack by a shadowy adversary. If we termed that uncertain threat a war, we had a clear and comfortable response: the Pentagon and its warfighting capability. A self-proclaimed "war on terrorism" also became an easily understood rallying cry.

But confronting terrorism is not a war and calling it one takes us down the wrong path. America's warfighting capability is a different toolset designed for a different purpose. Wars are fought between the military forces of opposing nations and firepower matters. That is what our military forces are organized, trained, and equipped to do.

Terrorism is a criminal act committed to achieve some political goal. The more criminal the act the better, the more vulnerable the target the better because the real objective is usually the resolve of a government. Inflict pain to change a policy. So an airplane is blown up in flight over Scotland in retaliation for economic sanctions against Libya, children are massacred in Chechnya to gain political separation from Russia, and iconic buildings in New York and Washington are attacked with hijacked airliners to compel the withdrawal of Western influence from Saudi Arabia. Invading Iraq had little to do with meeting the threat of terrorism.

Treating terrorism as a war will often make the situation worse. Terrorists are criminals, not heads of state. Declaring war on them gives them a stature they could never achieve on their own. In an internet-connected world, the fame and status of being on one side of a war against the United States is beyond value to the terrorists. It allows them to recruit forces, raise funds, and harvest hate against America. They don't have to make the case for their stature, we make it for them every time a president uses the phrase "global war on terror."

Wars break things. A military response to terrorism will often do more harm than good, will often kill more civilians than actual terrorists. Our standoff precision weapons—cruise missiles, smart bombs, and unmanned aerial vehicle–delivered missiles—make it easier to kill people, but also make it harder to know who we are killing. Each dead civilian non-combatant creates a family of new enemies committed to fighting Americans for generations to come. If we treat terrorism as a war, the numbers are against us.

Military force can have an important role to play in combating terrorism, but it is a role that requires careful thought. When the

Taliban regime in Afghanistan harbored the terrorists that conducted the September 11th attacks, the United States deployed primarily special operations forces and intelligence teams to support the anti-Taliban faction in northern Afghanistan. The important issue was not the firepower of the American military assets sent, but rather the support of an indigenous anti-Taliban force. Quite literally, a poorly trained Afghan crew in a barely running, 1950s vintage Russian tank was of more value than state-of-the-art American tanks spearheading a precision warfare military campaign. The Soviet Union fought the same Afghan enemy on the same terrain for a decade and lost. We fought for thirty days and helped roll back the Taliban influence in key parts of Afghanistan. The difference was that the Soviets were an occupying power, while we were supporting a homegrown Afghan force trying to displace a repressive theocracy. The Soviets were using military power to try to control a country and over the long term that seldom works. We were using limited and focused military assistance to support a legitimately indigenous effort. That stark difference can continue to guide, and to limit, America's efforts in Afghanistan and elsewhere.

In the final analysis, the United States will not defeat terrorism with military force. We will defeat terrorism with our values. The United States became a country, then a world power, then a super-power because of its commitment to freedom. That idea continues to spread to other nations, and free nations do not tolerate terrorists. In combating terrorism, America's soft power assets are more useful than our military muscle. These soft power assets—diplomacy, intelligence gathering, law enforcement support, and economic assistance—are of more value than the combat power of our weapons systems. Afghanistan makes that clear. Military power there gained only a pause, an opportunity for a government other than the Taliban to gain popular support. That government's performance will determine the outcome. Our soft power assets support the things that help a challenged government succeed.

PART II
THE WAY AHEAD

CHAPTER 4:
The Next Strategy

THE WAY AHEAD IS NOT STRAIGHT AHEAD. To renew the military might that America needs, we must craft a new defense strategy and build precision warfare forces to execute that strategy. We must re-tether our military to our people and rebalance our military between standing forces and citizen soldiers. We must reform the way we make decisions in the Pentagon, understand our role as a global power, and rethink defense funding. We must have better leadership from our generals, admirals, and presidents. Our senior military officers must again offer the independent military counsel that is critical to defense decision making. We will be well advised to have some idea what our next war is likely to be and how we can fight and win that war. There are solutions to these challenges if we are both bold and smart in grasping them.

All of that starts with a coherent defense strategy. Since the end of the Cold War, the United States has chased events rather than pursued a strategy. That makes wars both more likely to occur and more difficult to win. As we move beyond the Iraq War, we have the opportunity to think through how, why, and when we fight wars.

A successful defense strategy comes from identifying the threat, evolving a strategy to meet that threat, then building the forces to execute the strategy. George Marshall did that in World War II. The army in the 1930s assessed the likely threats that America faced. A war against Japan was Plan Orange. Germany, Italy, and several other countries each had a separate war plan, each with its own color. The most likely future conflict seemed to be war against Germany and Japan and their allies: hence, the Rainbow series of war plans that envisioned a very large U.S. Army that did not yet exist for a war that had not yet begun.[1] War plans are never a perfect fit for an uncertain future, but they are a start.

When World War II came, Marshall was able to offer Roosevelt a sensible strategy: fight Germany first with a cross-channel invasion and a land and air campaign in the heart of Europe while conducting a limited naval and amphibious campaign in the Pacific. Marshall then set about building the forces to execute his strategy: an eighty-nine division army and a formidable army air force.

That same strategic process succeeded in the Cold War. The immediate threat was a Soviet invasion of Western Europe, with or without a nuclear strike against the homeland of the United States. The American strategy to meet that threat was to fight the Soviets when and where they came across the border. That strategy required a robust NATO alliance led by a large American force permanently stationed in what was formerly West Germany, ready to fight on short notice, and a devastating nuclear strike capability of our own. That strategy worked: war was deterred until the standoff was resolved by the implosion of the Soviet Union.

The strategy that we need now will best come from the same process that has worked in our past: identify the threat, devise a strategy to meet that threat, and then build the forces to execute that strategy. The threats that we currently face are major conventional wars, crises and small wars that can escalate into major wars, and the emerging threat of global terrorism.

Major wars matter. We won a country in the American Revolution, preserved that country through our Civil War, and defended America in two world wars in the twentieth century. Had we lost in any of those instances, there would not be a United States today, or at least not one that we would recognize. Each of those wars arrived unscheduled, and victory in each appears much more certain through the lens of history than it did at the time. Because major conventional wars are the "game over" threat to America, the Pentagon's core mission should be to fight and win them. With the tectonic shifts now occurring in the world—an expansive China, a resurgent Islam, and nuclear proliferation—America's ability to wage conventional war is a matter of some urgency.

The threat of small wars is that they can become large wars. The mission of containing that threat goes by several designations: peacekeeping, engagement, and nation building among them. By any name, it is a worthwhile effort: avoiding wars where we can is always a good idea. A small force in a constabulary role can prevent the need for large warfighting forces in the future. The American and NATO deployment to Bosnia in the mid-1990s staunched a small war in a volatile region where each of the combatants had big power sponsors—a scenario uncomfortably similar to the beginnings of World War I. The question is not whether we will face the need to contain crises, but rather how often and for how long and with how large a force. Successful interwar missions extend the time between wars.

Terrorism is a deadly threat, but it is not war. Terrorism is criminal acts aimed at civilian targets to change government policies. There is a role for military force in counter-terrorism, but that force must be highly targetable and highly targeted.

Each of these threats is fundamentally different, and each requires a response different in kind from the others. Conventional wars are armies fighting other armies: the strategic goal is seizing territory or destroying the opposing force. That is done with tanks and ships and war planes. The lethality of weapons systems matters a great deal. Our between-war missions deal with crises and small wars: the strategic purpose is avoiding a wider war, usually with a limited number of forces in a peacekeeping role. Counter-terrorism is preventing criminal acts against civilian targets: the strategic goal is to have a secure American homeland.

Matching the wrong response to a threat is a significant mistake. A series of American presidents have grandly declared wars on poverty, on crime, and on drugs. Those were not wars, of course, but only politicians borrowing the language for political purposes. Treating counter-terrorism as a war is a mistake. The first three weeks of the war in Iraq was a force-on-force matter, and America's military won that handily. Everything after the first three weeks was a counter-insurgency, and no amount of American military power could win that war. Only a committed, functioning Iraqi government that is able to win the support of the Iraqi people can do that.

Our troops in Vietnam came to understand that idea. Among the places where our advisory forces worked, and over time a growing part of the U.S. Army in Vietnam was advisory, you could often find posted on a wall the Lawrence of Arabia wisdom from World War I: "Do not try to do too much with your own hands. Better the Arabs do it tolerably than that you do it perfectly. It is their war, and you are to help them, not to win it for them."[2] John Kennedy came to understand that about Vietnam as well. Several months before his death, he pointedly said in a television interview about the Vietnamese: "In the final analysis, it is their war. They are the ones who have to win or lose it."[3]

The strategy to meet the threats we now face, like most good strategies, is straight forward: build the capability to fight and win major wars; use our forces between wars to contain crises and prevent wider wars; and, in a limited role, use our military forces to combat global terrorism. That seems obvious, but we are in fact not doing that now and there is little indication that we will. We are off course in building a strategy for a number of reasons, all of which must be taken into account if we are to succeed.

We are suffering a strategic hangover from the Cold War. Our strategy then called for a large army, in place and ready to be at war in a matter of hours and days. That approach was spectacularly successful at the time, but our next strategy must get beyond the thinking in cadence of our Cold War success. In the four decades of the Cold War, the Pentagon and the White House became institutionalized around the idea that we go to war with the army we have. That is wrong: every major war that America has fought and won was fought and won with citizen soldier armies raised and trained and equipped to fight that war.

There was no national army before the American Revolution—George Washington had to build and train and sustain one. At the start of the Civil War, there were sixteen thousand soldiers in the army: two million would fight for the Union, nearly a million for the Confederacy, before that war ended. From a sliver of an army, both John J. Pershing in World War I and George Marshall in World War II built armies of millions of citizens become soldiers.

We will have time to do that for our next major war. The Cold War shot clock has been turned off, but the Pentagon is still in a rush-to-war mindset. That creates barriers that need not exist. Our army units in World War II had two and a half years to train for the invasion of Europe, we had ten years to get it right in Vietnam, and the Iraq War may last longer than that.

We are ignoring our past success in fighting our wars with citizen soldier armies because of how we make decisions in the Pentagon. As we drew down our forces at the end of the Cold War, it became apparent that if one of the armed services gave up a mission, it gave up the funding that went with that mission. The active duty force retained the mantle and the budget priority of being our warfight force, between-war missions became an additional duty to the warfight, and the fact that we actually fight our major wars with citizen soldier armies did not merit even an afterthought. Pentagon turf defense substituted for historical perspective and strategic insight.

Our ability to build a successful strategy is also hampered by the fact that presidents and generals no longer make decisions based on mutual understanding and respect. George Marshall and Franklin Roosevelt fought and won World War II, a global conflagration waged by simultaneous campaigns in far-flung theaters. They met together frequently, made decisions, and then Marshall and the other uniformed service chiefs implemented those decisions. In World War II, there were a total of eight secretarial and assistant secretarial positions in the War and Navy Departments. By the time of Vietnam, there were fifty. Today, there are well over a hundred and the number is still growing.[4] The White House personnel office parcels out those positions. Political payback and political loyalty usually drive who gets the job.

Defense decision making by bureaucracy isn't working. Roosevelt and his senior military officers directed an army, navy, and army air force of over twelve million people fighting a determined enemy on a global scale—and they won. For the Iraq War, our national security policymaking bureaucracy tried to manage an American force of no more than 162,000 fighting an enemy that had no tanks, ships, or airplanes, in a single country, and they still made a series of policy mistakes that hampered the American effort.

What has changed is not the quality of our forces; they are as good as any we have ever had. What has changed is how we make decisions in Washington. Senior flag officers—the generals and admirals who understand wars, how to avoid them, and how to fight them—are now bureaucratically distanced from final defense policymaking. Meetings with presidents have become pro forma events that affix a public relations imprimatur to civilian-developed decisions. The crucial hard-edged counsel from senior officers, which presidents need, has been lost.

Building and executing our next strategy faces these hurdles. We must get beyond the lingering Cold War mindset that we go to war with the army we have, we must do better in the Pentagon than make decisions by turf defense, and we must reinvolve senior flag officers at the heart of go-to-war decisions.

There is a strategy that will work. The threats are major wars, small wars that can escalate, and the emerging threat of global terrorism. The strategy to meet that threat should be to put in place the capabilities that will allow us to field the forces we'll need to fight major wars, use our standing forces to contain small wars and crises, and meet the threat of terrorism with something other than brute combat power.

CHAPTER 5:

Precision Warfare

MIDWAY BETWEEN TACTICS AND STRATEGY, there is an operational level of war. America's current operational approach is precision warfare. Precision is as great a change to war as was the introduction of gunpowder. We have to get this change right.

To understand what is going on, picture a young American pilot in the seat of an Apache attack helicopter flying above the desert at 150 knots at an altitude of less than a hundred feet. He (or, importantly, she) is in his mid-twenties and has been in the army for three years. The helicopter he is flying is a marvel. It was built in the 1980s, but every year or so someone bolts on some item of new technology. The Apache has forward-looking infrared radar that lets the pilot see at night or through smoke or clouds. The targeting pod at the front of the helicopter is programmed to move with the co-pilot's flight helmet. When he moves his head, it moves its head—and the weapons systems connected to it.

Airplanes that shoot are not new: armed aircraft flew over the trenches in World War I. The magic of the Apache is not the guns on the helicopter as much as the computers on the helicopter. The screen for several of them sits just above the pilot's right knee. That screen makes him the most powerful twenty-something military commander since Alexander the Great.

The Apache pilot has knowledge that soldiers through the ages have lusted after. He knows exactly where he is. That gift comes from a global positioning system updated every second from navigation satellites. On the moving map display on his computer screen, he sees an icon for every American tank, armored personnel carrier, or truck on the battlefield. That cuts down on all-American or all-Coalition firefights. Because of an incredibly expensive array of satellites, and airborne surveillance and reconnaissance aircraft, he usually knows where the enemy is. Not where he was five minutes ago, but where he is *now*, at this instant, within a meter or two. If the enemy is moving, the Apache pilot knows in what direction, at what speed. What he sees with his own onboard sensors goes back into the same information network.

That gives the Apache pilot, the battalion commander, brigade commander, division commander, and corps commander watching all of this on their own computers some truly powerful options. If the target on the Apache screen is critical, such as an enemy commander, someone will call in a cruise missile from a surface ship, offshore submarine, or orbiting bomber. A somewhat less grand target will merit artillery fire or precision-guided bombs from an air force aircraft or a missile from a loitering unmanned aerial vehicle. Or the Apache can fly in range and engage the target with rockets, gunfire, or fire-and-forget Hellfire air-to-surface missiles, usually before the enemy even knows the Apache is in the neighborhood.

What the Apache pilot is doing—precision warfare—is the latest iteration in an increasingly complex progression of conflict that started somewhere around the time of the Roman phalanx two millennia ago. That phalanx was followed by cavalry, which was followed in turn by bowmen, then by heavy cavalry, then by the British formation of infantry squares against which Napoleon squandered an empire at Waterloo. Of more immediate impact was the rifled musket in the American Civil War that gave the infantry a killing range of up to four hundred meters. Since all warfare up to that time had involved people trying to get within sword or bayonet range of an enemy, the basics of land warfare were fundamentally altered—a fact the collective generalship of the Western world failed to recognize until several million infantrymen died in World War I.

The operational breakthrough of World War II was mechanized warfare, both on the ground and in the air. Armies took the power of the internal combustion engine and used it to power tanks, trucks, and airplanes. That is what we still do. The breakthrough of precision warfare is adding the power of information technology to mechanized warfare.

Information allows precision, and precision allows lethality. During World War II, the U.S. Army Air Forces would send up to a thousand bombers at a time to attack a single target. That massive air armada would drop bombs and hope for the best: there was a great deal of randomness in how many bombs got close to the target. One bomb in ninety hit what it was aimed at.[1] Then, everyone would guess what damage had been done and whether they needed to send another fleet of planes the next day or week or month. Losses of dozens of planes on these huge raids—each with an aircrew of ten—were not uncommon.

Precision warfare changed all that. By Desert Storm, we could send one stealth airplane out alone to attack one target and have confidence that we would get a hit more often than not. Satellite imagery gave us reasonably reliable intelligence on what damage was caused and whether we needed to re-attack. And we had very high confidence that the pilot, an aircrew of one, would get back safely.

Our precision-guided munitions and air campaigning have further improved since Desert Storm. We can now send out one bomber to handle multiple targets and expect direct hits. When the air force mistakenly hit the Chinese embassy in Belgrade during the Kosovo air campaign in 1999, it wasn't that the bombs went astray. They hit the building they aimed for, in fact hit it several times. They were just aiming at the wrong building.

That kind of precision is why, in his Apache helicopter barreling along above the desert, the young pilot can be forgiven for thinking of himself in terms of Alexander the Great.

Precision warfare is not just Industrial Age warfare done better. There are some fundamental changes involved. For centuries, the critical issue on the battlefield was mass. Battles developed in a familiar sequence. A general found out where the enemy army was by bumping into it. He then maneuvered the bulk of his forces—mass—to where he thought they ought to be. Then both sides fought until someone quit. The sequence was contact, maneuver, decisive attack.

Precision warfare has a different sequence. With all that information from the satellite constellation and airborne reconnaissance, we can now detect the enemy location in some detail before the shooting starts. The American commander then maneuvers smaller, more agile forces to where they need to be. That lets our forces bypass the enemy strengths and attack just his critical weaknesses, in several places and in different ways. The first engagement is more likely to be the decisive engagement. Mass is less important than speed and lethality.

Precision warfare is an overwhelming American military advantage. No other nation in the world has made the investments in technology and training to fight this kind of fight. Only the United States has the intelligence, surveillance, and reconnaissance assets required. Our information-driven economy has given us information-driven warfare. America dominates the information age economy and our lead in information-driven warfare is significant. But there has been a series of advantages like precision warfare throughout history: bowmen at Agincourt; the combination of infantry, artillery and cavalry by Napoleon; the concentration of tanks in the German blitzkrieg. All of these advantages were lost over time. Ours of precision will be as well.

One of the ways to manage that inevitable fall from operational dominance is to stay flexible in an often overlooked part of America's warfighting ability: doctrine. Doctrine is our playbook. Each of the American armed forces have complete, detailed doctrine. It spells out how we go about fighting battles and wars. Doctrine lets everyone know, on a crowded, busy, and dangerous battlefield, what is supposed to happen next. Events often don't follow the script, but even that uncertainty is a part of the plan.

It wasn't always that way. The Prussians developed the idea of doctrine in the nineteenth century. Prior to that time, whatever the commanding general thought when he woke up the morning of the battle was how things were done. That allowed the occasional—and only occasional—military genius to blossom: Napoleon and Grant come to mind. More often, the commanding general was drunk, fell off his horse, got lost, or was inconveniently killed. Before doctrine, poorly fought battles were more frequent than not.

The Prussians developed not only the idea of doctrine but, for the 1870 Franco-Prussian War, a general staff organization to write doctrine and execute it. That move raised the level of generalship markedly, on average: if it has tempered the prospects for flagrant genius, it has proven to be a fair exchange.

As the Pentagon writes precision doctrine, there are some opportunities. It may seem obvious after you say it, but the military mission in wartime is not to kill every enemy soldier on the battlefield. The mission is to render the enemy ineffective as a fighting force. Viewed that way, precision warfare gives us some options that are more effective than those that just produce body counts.

In Desert Storm, the first set of targets was the Iraqi command and control system. Most dictators come to power and remain in power by military force. They then tend to keep their military units on a very tight rein to prevent some ambitious colonel from taking that same path to power. But the battles to which military forces are committed are both unpredictable and fast paced. During Desert Storm, if an Iraqi colonel was waiting for an order from Baghdad before moving a platoon of tanks, he probably ended up being overtaken by events. If his communications system to Baghdad was gone and the order to move that platoon never came, the war certainly passed him by.

During Desert Storm, maneuver was able to exploit precision warfare. In addition to a very one-sided air campaign, the Iraqi Army faced a looming American ground attack. Iraqi soldiers dug in behind minefields and obstacles, their guns were pointed to their front. All day every day, they looked to their front. When they looked over their shoulder and saw an American unit between them and their rear area, which is to say, between them and a return home, their enthusiasm for fighting diminished rather quickly. Precision warfare agility took entire Iraqi formations out of the fight.

All of this precision warfare targeting and maneuvering must be combined in a coherent campaign plan. Field Marshal Ferdinand Foch, the Allied commander in World War I, is often quoted as having said that it takes fifteen thousand dead to train a major general. If that was true, it was a devastating comment on the level of generalship they had and were looking for. Today, American generals must orchestrate a wide and complex range of precision combat capabilities under the eye of an unblinking global media and an equally unblinking command and control system reaching back to Washington. The expectation is for complete victory in a matter of hours or days with few or no casualties. Those expectations are often unrealistic, but precision brings us as close as we are likely to get.

Precision warfare also lets us deal with some peculiarly American operational issues. We are judicious now in bombing an adversary's infrastructure because we assume that the United States will pay to rebuild it after the war. Our enemies put their critical air defense assets near religious or humanitarian sites, confident that the United States will risk increased American military casualties to avoid increased enemy civilian casualties. Precision helps us make targeted attacks that will preserve infrastructure and civilian life while defeating the enemy force.

Our choice of precision warfare has extended the dimensions of the battlefield: space is now critical terrain because space is the ultimate high ground. Soldiers always want to own the top of the hill, because it lets them see and shoot at anyone or anything in sight. Airplanes are an extension of the hill, valuable for many of the same reasons. Space is the final high ground, important for the same reasons as hills and airplanes. It is not by chance that the Soviet Union felt it had to have a robust space program or that China feels so now. As we continue to transform our military forces into a precision warfighting force, putting weapons in space becomes an issue.

In a broad sense, space has already been weaponized. Our space-based intelligence, surveillance, and reconnaissance assets are the linchpin of our warfight. When America's adversaries have the ability to put weapons in space, they will. Because America is the most data-dependent military in the world, we have the most to lose if we are denied the use of our satellite constellation. We should be very concerned that China has demonstrated its ability to destroy low-orbit satellites with surfaced-launched missiles. They are certainly concerned that we can. When the United States shot down its own malfunctioning satellite in early 2008, China protested and asked for the data to be made public.

The rate of technological advances in this arena is exponential. Speed and data processing capacity, miniaturization, and materials research leverage off one another. As we move from kinetic energy weapons—things that explode—to directed energy weapons—like lasers—lethal weapons in space become more practical. There will be an arms race in space. If such matters could be settled by diplomats, the Kellogg-Briand Pact in 1928 would have outlawed war, there would have been peace in the Middle East decades ago, and there would today be a country called South Vietnam. The issue is not whether there will be an arms race in space, but who will win it. Building and deploying space weapons is not the answer. The solution is to watch what our adversaries are doing and stay ahead of them in the laboratory and with prototype testing. Those are American strengths. Our aerospace generals talk about avoiding a space Pearl Harbor and we should listen to them.

Precision warfare is our short-term future. It was and is the right choice for America, but we must not let it blind us. The Maginot Line built by the French prior to World War II was state-of-the-art technology. It used underground rail transport, protected crew quarters, and underground power stations. It was just the wrong technology.[2] In our past wars, our tactics have had to be changed, discarded, or reinvented once the shooting started. That is true of all armies and it can be an advantage for America as long as we have smart leaders, flexible doctrine, and soldiers of individual initiative.

None of our previous victories in war came through things that were mechanical. Before the beginning of Desert Storm, one of our division commanders said that he would give Saddam's army our equipment, take their equipment, and still beat them.[3] Our victories come from going to war for compelling causes, from finding gifted leaders, from honoring sound values, from the broad support of our citizens, and from going to war to defend America's freedom. Precision warfare works within that framework but does not work as a substitute for the more fundamental sources of our past victories.

CHAPTER 6:
The Next Force

WE ARE BUILDING THE NEXT AMERICAN MILITARY NOW. The Pentagon calls the change "transformation," a term that overstates the case. What we are doing is updating our Cold War army, navy, and air force with better technology and equipment to support our current needs. We are moving to an army that is more deployable, a navy that is network-centric, and an air force that has more-capable airplanes.

Change does not come easily in the American military. We have maneuver corps in our army in the twenty-first century because Napoleon had maneuver corps in his army in the early nineteenth century. Corps formations were a breakthrough for Napoleon, because they gave him a self-contained unit for his *levee en masse* armies. It is not the breakthrough for us now that it was for Napoleon.[1] Military organizations do not change easily or gracefully but our army is, in fact, changing.

To understand the change that is underway, a starting point is that the United States had a Cold War military strategy of confronting a massive Soviet armor attack coming east to west across Central Europe. The idea was that ten divisions of our active duty army, along with many more NATO divisions, would absorb the initial Soviet onslaught while U.S. National Guard divisions hurried into combat as reinforcements. The challenge was to not get kicked off the continent for the thirty or sixty days we thought it would take America to mobilize for war. Battles are talked about on a broad scale but are fought by individual soldiers, tanks, and planes. The Soviets had many more tanks than we did, less capable ones, but a lot of them. If the American strategy was to work, it meant as a practical matter that individual American tanks had to be able to take a hit from a Soviet tank and survive to keep fighting.

That simple fact started an armored volume spiral. To survive a hit, a certain amount of space inside a tank requires armor protection. In our army, four larger-than-average-size eighteen- to twenty-two-year-old American males had to fit inside that protected space, along with their ammunition and fuel. So we built our tanks to that size and standard and the battlefield tactics underlying our strategy appeared likely to work.

The Soviets were a learning enemy. They put a bigger main gun on their tanks, which gave them a bigger tank round that could penetrate our armor. So we went to thicker armor, which meant more weight. Then we put our own bigger gun on our tanks, which meant still more weight. We also got bigger tank rounds in the bargain, which was good, but bulkier rounds required more protected volume. All that extra weight for more armor, bigger guns, and bigger tank rounds required a bigger engine, which meant more fuel, more protected volume, and thus even more weight.[2]

When we were done, we had the best tank in the world . . . but it weighed seventy tons. More than half of that weight was for crew protection and survivability. Moving those leviathans about was a challenge. The United States rebuilt a significant number of the bridges on what we thought of as our side of the inter-German border. We fielded a large and complex logistics system to support our mechanized formations. All of that was difficult and expensive but it was the right strategy, well implemented, and we and our allies succeeded in deterring war in Europe.

Our current heavy force is leftover from the Cold War and that causes some fundamental problems. We have changed our strategy from being forward deployed—meaning our tanks were already located within driving distance of the battlefield—to being a power projection force, which means we must use ships and planes to get to a battlefield somewhere. Cold War tanks and infantry fighting vehicles are too heavy to be readily deployable. Our transportation corps soldiers say with undisguised pride that nothing happens until something moves. They are being modest: within a power projection strategy for a logistically complex force, nothing happens until almost everything moves. The everything part of that equation is important: the job of tank turret mechanic sounds like an obscure calling unless you are a tank commander with a broken turret.

A decade after the Cold War ended, the army's senior leaders set about shifting from a heavy force that could absorb a Soviet onslaught to something lighter, more agile, and more deployable. The army is initially adding some newly equipped brigades to cover the current gap between our heavy and light forces. We have great light infantry units. They can quickly deploy anywhere but lack the staying power necessary to withstand an armor attack. We have great heavy forces, the remnant of our Cold War force, but they are slow to deploy and require a massive logistics tail. The interim, mid-weight force will initially fill that gap.

The thought is that this interim force will continue to develop and eventually replace the heavy force. That move will require a step up in lethality. The technology that will allow us to replace the heavy force doesn't exist yet but the framework for it does: precision warfare that exploits information technology and using precision munitions, precision maneuver, and precision logistics.

To do all that, we need a vehicle formerly known as a tank. It will use low observable technology and hit avoidance rather than hit survivability. It will shoot something at enemy targets without having to stand face-to-face with them like an Old West gunfight. When the army decided to move to a more deployable force, two years of angst ensued over whether the future combat platform would have wheels or tank treads. If it didn't have treads, it could not be a tank and if it wasn't a tank, what was it?

Napoleon would have smiled.

Change in our army raises some important issues. The army appears standard from the outside, but it is not. If you are a division commander with thirteen battalions in your division, those battalions will not have identical equipment and computer systems. In a precision warfight, that inconsistency is important. If you are a president and send brigade combat teams to the Iraq War, no two of them will have fully the same equipment (although they are supposed to). This lack of uniformity comes about because we are constantly fielding new equipment and systems and, due to budget and operational constraints, it is nearly impossible to field them army-wide at the same time. So when a unit deploys, a portion of its equipment or vehicles will be new. Drivers and mechanics may not be trained to drive and maintain them. Some computer systems will be just out of the box. Leaders may not be fully aware of the new capabilities they have or the old capabilities they may not have. Leaders at every level have to find work-arounds for incompatibility issues.

The army is fixing this problem by becoming more modular, which is to say more standard. Change is required, but those changes have to be thought through by warfighters, not budgeteers: even modest glitches can have a big impact on seemingly unrelated areas in our tightly connected precision combat capabilities.

From Theodore Roosevelt's Great White Fleet to the later years of the Cold War, the base capability of the U.S. Navy was to go to sea and keep sea lanes open. For much of the Cold War, that strategy remained more or less unchallenged. But in the 1970s, the Soviets began building a truly oceangoing navy that could interdict the American sea-based rush to war in Europe. That Soviet capability put a new light on all matters naval and strategic.

To meet the Soviet threat, the U.S. Navy shifted to a strategy of placing our fleet in European littoral waters. We were going to put our ships close enough to the Soviet Union to threaten their homeland, a change that injected our ships and naval aviation aircraft into prospective Cold War land and air battles. The navy called its strategy, perhaps somewhat theatrically, From the Sea. That was a bold plan and whether the navy would have actually tried such a high-risk option is an open question. Aircraft carriers have a historic and well-founded aversion to close-in waters and the land-based aircraft and missiles found there. But the navy intended to employ the From the Sea strategy and the Soviets were convinced we would come inshore: they then altered their own naval strategy to pull their fleet back in toward their home waters. That is where matters stood when the Cold War ended.

Things are again changing. The navy remains platform-centric, meaning they think in terms of ships and planes, but a change is underway to make the navy network-centric, to tie together the navy's range of combat power into a more coordinated warfighting capability. From their forward deployed position at sea, the navy plans to approach a hostile shore with a cohesive array of missiles, marines, and airplanes. They will pull data from sensors and form knowledge from information on the network.

The navy has a network-centric class of surface vessels on the drawing boards. These ships are stealthy and have more computers and fewer crew members. They are designed to fight with information-driven intelligence and precision. The navy is also building a class of littoral combat ships that can be reconfigured with different equipment modules for different missions.

The speed of response possible through information technology will let the navy get inside an adversary's decision cycle. During the air war run-up to Desert Storm, it took three days to plan a cruise missile attack. For the Kosovo air campaign in 1999, it took ninety minutes. During the Iraq War, the navy adjusted its targeting after the missiles were already launched.

Our adversaries know full well that we are a power projection force and that we are most vulnerable while moving forces into theater. That vulnerability is somewhat akin to straddling a fence: at some point in every deployment, we will have enough forces in the war theater to be a lucrative target but not enough forces to be a balanced fighting force. The navy, in addition to its mission of keeping sea lanes open, can help fight the anti-access fight for the rest of the follow-on forces. Once everyone is ashore, the navy and marines will stay committed to the land and air campaign.

In the late 1960s, American analysts picked up glimmers of intelligence that the Soviets were building a breakthrough new fighter that could beat the American F-4 Phantom, at the time the best aircraft we could get in the air. That was an era, it now seems hard to recall, when we expected to battle the Soviet Air Force in the skies over Europe if not over the United States. To stay in the air interdiction fight, the air force designed and fielded the F-15. As it turned out, the Soviet fighter, the MiG-25 Foxbat, wasn't all that good. The F-15 was.

The F-15 is a heavy airplane that has two engines, lots of electronics, and a lethal array of rockets that can shoot down other airplanes. It is still a good air-to-air fighter, particularly when flown by American pilots, who receive far and away the best training in the world. But the F-15 is no longer dominant. The plane is based on 1960s technology, albeit with upgraded electronics. Age and metal fatigue have led to aircraft breaking apart in flight and to periodic groundings of the F-15 fleet. Technology, both the things that go in such planes and the things that are used in designing and building them, has moved light-years forward since the F-15 was fielded in 1972. Our air-to-ground aircraft, the F-16, is fast approaching the same problems. Its design was completed and production began in 1975.

One of the clearest lessons learned from Desert Storm was that having the second-best air force in a conflict, even second-best by a small margin, is a losing proposition. An air force that has an edge for whatever reason—aircraft performance, pilot skill, maintenance-driven on-station availability, or air refueling capability—will win the pass/fail exercise of air combat.

The successor aircraft to the F-15 and the F-16 fleet are the F-22 and the F-35 Joint Strike Fighter. They are the heart of the next U.S. Air Force. First, the F-22. If you are flying an air-to-air combat mission in an F-15, a pilot in the most current Soviet-built fighter, the SU-33 and its progeny, has a longer-range missile than you do and can shoot at you before you can shoot at him. If you are in an F-22, because you are in a radar-avoiding stealth aircraft, the exact opposite is true. You see the Soviet fighter well before he sees you, and you can shoot at him before he knows you are in that air space.

As our adversaries field increasingly capable air defense systems, the better ground-to-air missile launchers are clumped together in something called double-digit SAMS, which are the more capable surface-to-air missiles. In an F-15, the double-digit SAMs can shoot you down. In an F-22, you get to shoot at them and turn for home before they can acquire you as a target. The turn for home part is important because, if you miss with your shot, they don't have a missile that can catch you from behind.

The argument for the Joint Strike Fighter (JSF) is also persuasive. In the 1960s, Secretary of Defense McNamara tried to make the air force, navy, and marines all buy the same fighter, called the TFX. It was a good idea, but the state of technology at the time would not support the concept. The breakdown came over something as mundane as weight. Since the TFX idea failed, the Pentagon bought and fielded the F-15, F-16, and A-10 in the air force; the F-14 and F-18 in the navy, and the F-18 and the Harrier in the marine corps. Those six very different airplanes came with six mostly different maintenance tails. Each support tail is something on the order of four to five times the size of the combatant plane and pilot units. That is a lot of duplicated force structure and budget.

Technology can now support a common platform for much of our aircraft needs. About 80 percent of the JSF is the same for the plain vanilla air force version, the stout undercarriage navy carrier version, and the marine vertical takeoff and landing version. Metal has given way to composites that are stronger but only a fraction of the weight of the metal parts they replace. Flight tests have traditionally been inherently dangerous because pilots and plane builders were testing new ideas by flying them: once the data was collected, someone would bend metal to try to make the airplane fly better. The computer design capabilities now used in building aircraft have made flight tests less a life-and-death event and more a validation of what the computer tweaked before the aircraft was built in the first place. The array of computers now routinely onboard our top-end aircraft open up performance envelopes that simply did not exist before: pilots operate the computers, the computers fly the airplane.

There are two main technology directions in the air power business: stealth and precision. Stealth changes everything. The United States is on its fourth or fifth generation of stealth technology. No one else has fielded their first. Our lead in precision is just as great: we have a precision-enabling constellation of satellites that far outpaces any other nation's surveillance capability.

The next air force is a linear step forward from our current air force. It is new planes plugged into a precision warfare framework.

Transformations are hard. Military transformations normally arise from desperate threats to the nation. In the brief years of World War II, American military aviation went from just out of biplanes to testing jet fighters. Self-generated transformations like the ones we are engaged in now have been less successful. The last major army transformation occurred during the early stages of the Cold War and was called the Pentomic Division. Bureaucratic enthusiasm and the Pentagon budget were advancing the role of air power and nuclear weapons. To catch up with the air force and navy, the army decided to reorganize into five-sided divisions. The Pentomic division had five major maneuver units and fielded tactical nuclear weapons down to a very low level, to include individual nuclear artillery rounds and backpack nukes. The idea was that the Pentomic division could fight and survive on a nuclear battlefield. The army bought something called the Davy Crockett missile that launched a nuclear warhead, but not farther than a mile and a quarter, thus having the potential to kill the enemy and the Americans that fired it with the same shot.[3] That all may seem silly now, but at the time, with the Cold War in full force and nuclear weapons all the rage, it made some sense.

The Pentagon is doing better with the current transformation, but there are still some issues to be addressed. Transformation means something different to admirals and generals than it does to civilians. Senior officers who have responsibility for fighting wars talk about tradition. The things that have worked in previous wars are real. Civilians who have responsibility for budgets talk about skipping technology generations, occasionally overlooking the fact that day-to-day missions remain while we transform to a new force. Transforming the forces that are currently defending the nation is very much like working on an aircraft while it is in flight. It can be done, but it has to be done with care and thought.

Our next army, navy, air force, and marines should move to the next level of joint warfighting. One of the reasons that the landing at Normandy in World War II was so precarious was that our land, sea, and air forces were fighting largely separate battles. There was an air bombardment plan and a naval gunfire plan and a land force maneuver plan. Any connection among them was lost when the first shots were fired. The air and sea bombardments missed their targets, but there was no way for the army forces on the ground to tell that to the navy and air force, much less to adjust those fires to get them on target. The army ashore had no radios that could talk to the air and naval shooters, nor doctrine or training to allow them to do so even if a workable communications capability had been in place.

A very keen army air force general fixed that fire support coordination problem after Normandy. For the Allied campaign across France, Belgium, and Holland into Germany in 1944–45, Major General Pete Quesada placed air corps pilots with radios that could talk to airplanes with the advancing army infantry and armor units.[4] The pilots set afoot were apparently as keen as their general: Quesada had more volunteers for the mission than he had slots to fill.[5] The army was able to adjust air strikes in the ensuing critical battles.

That is how we still do business today, managing the efforts of our land, sea, and air forces at the seams where they bump up against each other. A seam occurs when the navy or air force drops bombs in support of ground maneuver units, when air defense coverage in coastal areas is provided by Aegis-equipped navy ships, or when the army uses helicopter gunships or special operations teams to take out enemy air defense systems so that navy and air force aircraft can have a free hand. Our current goal is to have a coordinated battle, what the Pentagon calls "seamless." We are not there yet, but we do much better now than we did at Normandy.

The next force should step up to the next level of jointness, a level beyond seam management. We must move to a joint warfight where we think and plan and fight the same battle, not just manage separate battles. We need to move to a "born joint" warfight where our battlefield capabilities are designed as joint from their inception. There are some hurdles to be overcome before we can reach a born joint level of warfighting.

The first hurdle is also one of our greatest strengths: the individual military services. No recruits raise their hands and join the Department of Defense. They join the army or the navy or the air force or the marines. The services are the ballast of our warfight. They recruit, train, and equip our forces. They develop doctrine, train leaders, and safeguard leader ethics. The warfighting culture and traditions of the services run deep. The Department of Defense deals with budgets and does even that badly. The challenge is to capture the full power of the joint warfight without degrading the strengths and traditions of the services. We can do that, can move to the next level of jointness, by using the services' own internal dynamics.

The four military services hang on surprisingly similar frameworks. All have service doctrine, their playbooks. All the services have unit organizations defined by function. They all have incessant training. All of the services have equipment that they update. All have extensive leader development programs. The services are always evolving—at glacial speed in some areas, but still evolving. We can identify joint warfighting requirements and meet those requirements by adjusting the services' doctrine and training and equipping efforts.

There is, for example, a joint requirement for deep strike fire support missions from naval vessels. So army battalion commanders need to know how to do that. The army can add a page to their doctrine playbook for naval deep strike and then add a block of instruction at the army's lieutenant colonels' school, the Command and General Staff College at Fort Leavenworth. That lets future army battalion commanders know there is something out there called naval deep strike and that they have to know how to plan it and use it and coordinate it with their other fire support assets. The navy, in the meantime, at its similar course at Newport, lets their future ship captains know that the army will be calling. Then the Pentagon includes naval fire support in battalion and higher war games for the army and fleet exercises for the navy. When he gets to his battalion command, the army lieutenant colonel finds a new software module for naval deep strike options in his automated planning process. The navy ship captain's onboard planning and fire control system has a similar, and compatible, capability. The army lieutenant colonel and the navy captain are already getting data from and pushing data through the same satellites.

Everybody keeps wearing their own uniform. The army is still the army and the navy is still the navy. We use the existing service strengths to meet a joint warfighting requirement. We can capture the requirements for joint operations across the board and roll them back into the service dynamics. That will give us a born joint warfight.

The best way to understand what we are trying to do, to understand the power of the joint warfight, is to add it all up. That starts with a soldier with a rifle.

An infantryman can shoot his weapon on semiautomatic fire, which is to say one shot at a time, and hit something at about two hundred meters. Beyond that distance, the line infantryman will miss more often than not. He can also fire his weapon on full-automatic, a burst of shots for as long as he holds the trigger back and has rounds in his weapon. That will make him feel better and may make the enemy keep his head down, but his chances of hitting anything on purpose beyond one hundred meters are slim. Our infantryman can walk most of the day at 2.5 miles an hour if we can avoid loading him down with equipment. By the time all the good ideas from higher headquarters get to him, he has something on the order of 150 pounds of gear to lug around. That is too much by half, so he ends up sorting through the good ideas and taking with him the things he thinks will keep him alive and comfortable.

If we put our infantryman in an armored personnel carrier, good things begin to happen. He can then move at twenty-plus miles an hour, take all 150 pounds of gear someone thought he needed, and he has a heavy machine gun or 25mm cannon on the personnel carrier to give him some fire support. The armor part of the armored personnel carrier isn't like the armor protection of a tank, but it is a lot better than nothing.

If we put the personnel carrier with an M1-A2 Abrams tank, some other good things happen. The Abrams can reach out several thousand meters with an array of main gun rounds. The tank or truck that can stand up to those rounds hasn't yet been invented. Now add artillery, because Americans like to expend artillery rounds rather than soldiers' lives. So our combined arms task force can move far and fast, logistics allowing, and go toe-to-toe with any ground force that exists.

If we include helicopter gunships and air force and naval aviation in the mix, things get even better. Close air support extends the range of the ground force dramatically. Having the ability to reach out and touch your enemy behind his frontline is crucial because it prevents him from getting the daily resupply he needs to maintain combat power and usually induces him to move his frontline back. If the enemy force moves back with enough spontaneity, it is called a retreat.

Include precision. The information available from the current space-based and airborne intelligence, surveillance, and reconnaissance systems increases our warfighting potential significantly. One round placed exactly where you want it is worth dozens of rounds somewhere in the vicinity. Better, in fact, because you didn't have to haul all those extra rounds to the always-distant battlefield or maintain the support and logistics systems to get them in the air so they could miss the target.

Add it all up. The infantryman is the building block, but he is a lot more powerful mounted and sent into battle with tanks and artillery. Our ground fight capability doubles or triples with close air support, in addition to the bonus of isolating the battlefield to keep the enemy from resupplying his own forces. Make all that movement and shooting more precise, and you reach a level of lethality that is the unfair fight—unfairly to our advantage—that we seek.

The next army will be more deployable, the navy will be more networked, and the air force will fly more-capable aircraft. Those forces should be truly joint. Those are the forces we need to prepare to fight conventional wars, contain small wars and crises, and deal with the emerging threat of counter-terrorism. What is more important than the specifics of the forces we build is that we build them within the fundamental framework of our previous success.

We are not doing that. We have mistakenly assumed that the forces we have now will fight our next major war. They will not. We must re-tether our military to our people and then rebalance our forces between the interwar standing forces we have now and the citizen soldier warfighting force we will need to build.

CHAPTER 7:
Re-tether the Force

We must reconnect the American military to the American people. That connection will get us back inside our history, back inside how our government is supposed to work, and it will allow us to raise the forces we will need when the next major war finds us.

There are several ways to re-tether our soldiers and citizens, and the shared values of military service is a good place to begin. When you report in to army or marine boot camp, they cut off your hair, take away your civilian clothes, and drop you into a bewildering rush of seemingly senseless tasks and yelling drill sergeants. They stress your body to the breaking point by physical conditioning and arduous training. Every minute of every day and night, week after week, is scheduled in crushing detail. The idea is to strip away years of hanging out and sleeping late. As those cobwebs are swept away, a rebuilding can begin that gives civilians the capacity to be soldiers.

That rebuilding is captured by what used to be obstacle courses. These are cleverly designed towers and pits and things that must be climbed over or crawled under. Some of them have machine guns firing just overhead, others have explosions detonating at the moment you crawl or run by. These courses are purposely laid out to challenge the trainee's sensible fears of heights and falling and getting shot. If you are not afraid going though one of these courses, someone needs to redesign the course. They are not called "obstacle courses" anymore, they are called "confidence courses."

That is the thrust of the boot camp and beyond rebuilding. It is mastering fear and pain in manageable slices. Every day, the physical demands get a little harder, the experiences a bit more frightening. Not a lot from the day before, but some, which adds up over months and years. Many people are not up to the demands. A third of our soldiers quit or are separated from service before they complete their initial enlistment, most for failing to meet standards. But those who do come out the other end are leaner and stronger both mentally and physically. They have the confidence for combat.

A less obvious but equally important part of the rebuilding process is to impart core values to our recruits: courage, integrity, and service to the nation, among others. Courage underlies much of what our people in uniform do. It is an infantry squad maneuvering into enemy fire, a single-pilot fighter challenging a heavy air defense system, a night landing on an aircraft carrier.

Moral courage is just as critical. It is doing the right thing for the right reasons regardless of the consequences. It is a deep level of authority that crops up in expected and unexpected places. It is a battalion commander telling his young infantrymen the day before their first battle that Americans really do take prisoners in an assault. It is a staff sergeant telling a four-star theater commander who has questioned his unit's combat capability: "Sir, do you know who you are talking to? This is the 101st Airborne."[1] It makes taking care of troops something called "soldier issues," and soldier issues trump headquarters regulations. Just a few soldiers of moral courage leaven a whole force.

Integrity is adhering to values. The troops do what they see their leaders do. A leader's commitment to values makes a unit successful. A leader's integrity can get a unit through combat, and that sears the worth of integrity into every soldier who watches it happen.

People in uniform talk less than civilians about service to the nation but live it more. It is an undertone. They are the keepers of

America's freedom; they know that and are proud of it. That sense of service and pride, instilled and protected by our leaders, is what drives our people to make the sacrifices they make.

The purpose of all this rebuilding is to have armed forces that can defend America. A close second on the benefit scale is that our people leave the military with core values shared among themselves, shared with the generations of soldiers who have come before them, and shared with the American people. Twenty-five million living Americans have served our country in uniform. Their shared values are a national asset.

In Washington, at the center of the National Mall, there is a memorial to the generation of Americans who fought and won World War II. These men and women are often called the "greatest generation" and that is a fair description. But in spite of their sacrifices, in spite of their success, most of that generation would tell you that they gained more from their service than they gave. The challenge now is to get more Americans serving the nation in some meaningful way. If they do, they will give a lot, but they also will benefit more than they give.

America should have a widely based national service program, six months or a year for young Americans to work for their country and their fellow citizens. That may or may not have to be mandatory: some mix of incentives and leadership might be sufficient. When John Kennedy started the Peace Corps, Americans joined because they were inspired by his vision and their vision of the role America could play in the world.

Some of those who serve will choose the military, and that is well and good. More will choose some form of service other than the military, and that is just as good. We need hands to tend to the needs of the environment, health care, and education: there is no shortage of work to be done. The country will benefit, but those serving will benefit even more. Once you have served the nation in some serious way and have learned the values that have made our country what it is, you begin to think like an equity owner in America.

America's military has been a key to national service in the past. In the early 1930s, the nation was in the depths of the worst economic depression in our history. A failed economy had ripped apart the fabric of tens of thousands of American families. For far too many, there were no jobs, little money, and less hope.

Enter Franklin Roosevelt, who would try almost any idea that reached his desk. As it happened, one of Roosevelt's early enthusiasms when he became president was to find a way to get America's left behind youth some chance at a future. He began the Civilian Conservation Corps (CCC), which took these bypassed young men out of the cities and sent them to live in camps in the woods and countryside. There they planted trees, built trails, and constructed access roads into national parks. While they worked on conservation, the CCC staff worked on them. They learned to get up early and work hard, to use tools, and many learned to read.[2] They found the structure and values and discipline that the Depression had denied them.

The task of organizing and running the CCC was monumental, and it fell to the army. The U.S. Army was not taken seriously by much of anyone at the time. From a World War I high of 2.5 million people, the army had shrunk to under two hundred thousand soldiers. Its equipment was obsolete, its officers and men underpaid. Even this scrap of an army was looking for a mission. Roosevelt gave them one. The army had at least one skill left in its institutional memory from the Great War: it could mobilize, care for, and train hundreds of thousands of young men. A narrow skill, perhaps, but just the one called for in Roosevelt's scheme. Mobilization began, camps were built, officers took charge. It worked and worked well. A generation was recaptured.

We can create that kind of change again and strengthen the bond between America and its citizens, but boldness will be required. The current AmeriCorps program puts about a thousand youths each year in camp and to work. In the 1930s CCC effort, more than 250,000 young Americans were in the program within ninety days of Roosevelt signing the legislation.[3]

The national service youth who choose a military option become the citizen soldiers of our next major war. This is not militarizing our civilians, it is civilianizing our military. The purpose of our military is to deter war by being able to win wars. An American citizen soldier army defending American ideals is a far greater deterrent than the most technologically adept standing forces.

National service will also help correct a critical fissure that divides most of America from those who fight our wars. Through World War II, people from all parts of America went to war when war came. That is no longer the case. We do not want to become an army where the number of recruits and their background are determined by the size of an enlistment bonus.

We are already using our military resources, values, and traditions to help some young Americans who need help badly. There are programs in more than half the states called Youth Challenge. The National Guard in those states takes kids who have few opportunities and gives them a realistic chance for a better future. These are high school dropouts who are usually one step ahead of the law. The Guard program takes them to a training site, most often on a military base. That gets them away from the temptations and trouble of their neighborhoods. In a military setting, they spend half of each day studying and the other half learning life skills and job skills. This is not a jail or a boot camp. Like the CCC, the only sanction is to tell them they have to leave. And like the CCC, they are exposed to core values.

Great things happen in these programs. After six months, these young men and women are all but unrecognizable as those who started the program. Most graduate with or are on track toward earning a GED, and each has a team of mentors waiting for them back in their communities. They stand taller, look you in the eye more, have a sense of self-respect. A year after graduation, most either have a job, are in college, or are in the military. Youth Challenge is a current version of the Civilian Conservation Corps. Every few years, someone in the Pentagon tries to end the program because it is deemed to not be a military mission. That is too narrow a reading of the mission. Youth Challenge weaves more strands in the tether between America and its military.

Youth Challenge is, and national service can be, a good investment purely from a dollar standpoint. The cost of the widely used GI Bill educational benefits given veterans after World War II was repaid to the U.S. government four times over by the increased taxes these veterans paid during their work careers.[4] That is not the only reason to have Youth Challenge or national service, but it should figure in the calculation somehow.

If the defense of America is to be every citizen's responsibility, that means *every* citizen. Anyone who wants to question the role of women in the military should run the Marine Corps Marathon held in Washington each fall. They will get to run 26.2 miles through the monuments and edifices of the nation's capital along with a lot of military people. They will also be outrun by hundreds, if not thousands, of women. Opinions on who can meet the rigors of infantry combat can be recorded at the finish line.

Disqualifying wholesale groups of people from any military mission is not smart. A better approach is to set standards, and let everyone who wants to be a part of the mission try. The standard is performance and that means taking your weapon and, in the mission description of the infantry, closing with and destroying the enemy. In the Iraq War, women did that under fire and did it quite well. Whether women can perform infantry close combat is no longer in question. How America deals with that fact, however, still is.

The issue of gays in the military seems to be a lot more important to people outside the military than it is to those still serving. Of the top ten things that will determine whether we win or lose the next war, how the military treats gays is nowhere on the list. The current policy of don't ask/don't tell was a compromise, an attempt to let gay soldiers serve without raising issues that undermine the good order and discipline that military units must have. Quite predictably, it did not satisfy the hardliners on either end of the debate.

We are not talking about gays or straights, men or women. We are talking about our troops. These are the young Americans our officers have taken responsibility for, who they train and feed and house and look after. Our leaders will take them into harm's way, where they will do incredible things. Looking after soldiers—all of our soldiers—is a basic part of our military culture. That core tenet outweighs sexual orientation and gender, hands down. If we stay true to our fundamental value of taking care of soldiers, the rest will sort itself out over time.

The American military routinely does something that the rest of America has not been able to do: be a colorblind meritocracy. Success in uniform depends on how well you fly an airplane, drive a ship, or hump a rucksack and fire a weapon. No one cares what color you are. There are exceptions to that pervasive standard but those exceptions are rare.

Military service has been a traditional avenue to a better life for American minorities, but that is changing as the entry standards for our all-volunteer force go up. There were periods in the Cold War and Vietnam where young criminal offenders were given the choice of jail or the military. A conscripted force encourages that kind of thinking. Today, the very offenses that earned some good soldiers the choice between jail or the army can keep people out of the army completely.

High standards for people entering military service are the right approach. Less-qualified recruits are a problem across the board. They take more training time and money, are more likely to cause discipline problems, and are much less likely to complete their tour. Higher-quality recruits bring the skills that our technology enabled precision warfight requires and the skills and good sense that our complex interwar engagement missions need.

For all of that, the increased recruiting standards for our all-volunteer force have narrowed who can serve. Three quarters of eighteen- to twenty-five-year-old Americans today do not meet the army's enlistment standards.[5] Some can get waivers for selected standards, but that is lowering the standards we thought they should have met. We may need to rethink what our standards are and how we set them. Somehow, a connection between our people and our army needs to get in the mix.

Our military must also include our more affluent and influential Americans. In both world wars, our elites went to war. Before America entered World War I, military training camps at Plattsburgh, New York, and elsewhere were filled with prominent citizens and students from prestigious universities who paid their own way to attend.[6] The Lafayette Escadrille, a volunteer aviation squadron, was the first American unit into combat and was, for all practical purposes, an Ivy League flying club. Beyond that, the Yale Aero Club purchased seaplanes and trained at their own considerable expense. When the Great War came, they joined the navy and almost doubled the size of America's naval aviation.[7]

America's elites again went to war in World War II. Just after Pearl Harbor, Senator Harry Truman was determined to go back into the artillery where he had served in World War I: his strongly pressed request was turned down in a personal meeting with General Marshall.[8] A Supreme Court justice, Frank Murphy, lobbied to go to war with Patton's new tank corps.[9] The 1940 Oscar winner Jimmy Stewart was in uniform by 1941 and would soon be flying combat missions in Europe.[10] Of 5,700 major and minor league baseball players, in an era when baseball really was the national pastime, 4,000 went into the military.[11] The entire starting lineup of the New York Yankees was in uniform by the time of the Normandy invasion.[12]

The trend from where we were to where we are is not good. For World War I, Ivy League students paid their own way to get military training. They were in the recruiting lines on December 8, 1941. After

Vietnam, the Reserve Officer Training Corps (ROTC) program was banned from Harvard. Now, prestigious universities sue the Pentagon to bar recruiters from campus.

Perhaps we should rethink how we define "elite." Only a quarter of young Americans meet the enlistment standards of our army. Of those that enlist, two-thirds complete their first enlistment. Of those, only 20 percent are combat soldiers. These young men and women may lack affluence, their families may lack influence, but they have made themselves elite by their actions. Think of that when you next see a soldier in an airport.

If we fight our wars with standing armies, we forfeit one of the critical sources of our past success: the bond between Americans and their military. If we re-tether our military to America, through shared values and through expanded service by more of our people, we renew one of our fundamental strengths. America's past victories have come from America's citizens deciding that war was required and then going to fight that war. Allowing presidents to send standing military forces to war starts wars we should not fight and does not prepare us for the wars that we will have to fight.

We need a fundamentally different defense structure than the one we have now. We need a capable, full-time force for the full-time interwar missions. We need a mix of our active duty and reserve component forces to comprise the weight of our warfight, and a large national service pool of citizen soldiers in the event of a major war. What we do now is spend almost all of our time, thought, and resources on having the best active-duty force. What we should do is use our standing force to prevent wars and as the base from which to expand to a citizen soldier army for the next major war.

CHAPTER 8:

Rebalance the Force

IF WE ARE TO RENEW OUR MILITARY MIGHT, we must rebalance our forces between our standing military and citizen soldiers. How we fill our ranks is not a manpower issue: it goes to the core of the nation we are.

Longfellow got it wrong. When Paul Revere rode out of Boston the night before the American Revolution began, he did not in fact say "The British are coming." Everyone at that point was still British. What he did say was, "The regulars are coming," meaning the regular British Army.[1] Many of the colonists, including many of those most inclined toward revolt, were citizen soldiers of the colonial militia. When they said "regulars," it was not a compliment. The distinction between standing forces and citizen soldiers is still worthy of attention. Each has historic roles that have served America well. Each has been critical to the success of American arms. They bring separate strengths in war and peace, and they are not interchangeable.

Throughout its history, America has fought its wars with citizen soldiers, armies raised and trained and deployed to fight those wars. In the American Revolution, the colonial militia evolved into the Continental Army. At the close of the Revolution, it became obvious that some full-time military force would be needed. On the day the Continental Army was disbanded, eighty full-time soldiers were retained on active duty to guard the stores left over from the war.

Seven hundred militiamen were soon called to active service for a year.[2] Tasks other than just guarding stores came along. As the frontier moved westward, there were Native Americans to fight. The military academy at West Point was founded as a school to train engineers: the expanding frontier had roads and bridges to be laid out and forts to be built and garrisoned.

The Civil War was fought by citizen soldier armies, by choice. Before the Civil War, the army consisted of little more than a corporal's guard of an army and most of them were from the wrong side of the tracks.[3] During the Civil War, nearly three million men would take up arms, men from all levels and walks of American life.[4] To maintain anything approaching the Civil War–sized force in peacetime would have been completely out of character with the nation America was and aspired to be.

As the twentieth century approached, two events came together that changed our standing military forces. The Spanish-American War attracted tens of thousands of volunteers who joined for the fight. Not many of them made it into combat, and the euphoria of winning a war at little cost cast a warm glow on all things military. The second and more important event was that America became a colonial power. The Philippines, Hawaii, Guam, Samoa, Puerto Rico, and Panama all fell or were snatched into the American portfolio. A lingering insurrection and occupation of the Philippines called for a large and long-term commitment of forces there. That mission was very different from citizen soldier warfighting; it was full-time garrisoning. America was building an empire and its army and navy became the builders.

The American Expeditionary Forces of World War I grew from a small standing army to two million citizen soldiers in France. The weight of that force meant victory for the Allies. The military model of the Civil War was re-created: regular officer senior leadership, a core of regular soldiers, and large formations of citizen soldiers. In World War II, our army and army air corps grew from a prewar total of fewer than two hundred thousand to more than eight million.

The fact that we fight our major wars with citizen soldier armies is self-evident, but we lost sight of that wisdom during the Cold War. During much of that era, in an area of central Germany, the U.S. Army manned a series of unusual structures. They resembled two-story beach houses raised on very solid, very tall posts. One side of the structures had half-height walls, the better to see to the east. That unobstructed view across the German countryside usually included a concrete Soviet watchtower complete with an East German soldier looking malevolently back. These American towers—and there were a lot of them fortifying the border between the two Germanys—dotted an unbroken belt of minefields and high barriers of barbed wire. This was the rural extension of the Berlin Wall, a heavily armed military zone that separated the democratic west from the communist Soviet bloc east.

These American outposts were the tip of the spear. Located not far behind the towers were company alert positions. There, tanks and armored personnel carriers stood ready, crews ate and slept and waited just steps from their vehicles. They could move into position near the towers, full up and fighting, in a matter of minutes. Behind them were battalions, brigades, divisions, corps, and field armies. These units all had routes of eastward advance mapped and planned and rehearsed. The Soviets had their own massed formations of troops behind their watchtowers. Their routes of advance all pointed west.

In the American military, strategy drives requirements. Our strategy was to fight the Soviets when and where they came across the border. That required a big army, in place, ready to fight. For the first time in its history, the United States maintained a large army of conscripted soldiers in peacetime. The draft became an accepted part of the Cold War.

The war was going to start in the Fulda Gap, where we thought the Soviets would come across the West German border. The Fulda Gap became the centerpiece of our operations orders. Successive generations of corps and division commanders took their brigade and battalion commanders to the Fulda Gap, walked the ground and set out exactly where each unit would be on which piece of terrain. Gun positions were plotted, fields of fire planned, resupply routes coordinated.

It was all going to happen very quickly. We would have ten divisions in theater in ten days. Four divisions were already stationed in Germany and another six full division sets of equipment were stored there, ready for soldiers to fly from the United States to mount their tanks, trucks, and armored personnel carriers and move out. Those division equipment sets were a marvel. They took years of budget hoarding to accumulate and were maintained in top mechanical condition inside climate-controlled hanger-like buildings. It was an eerie spectacle: the equipment for an entire army waiting patiently for that army to get there.

The headquarters for this army were still in the buildings that had been summarily appropriated from the defeated Germans after World War II. We had a theater headquarters, an army headquarters, two corps headquarters, and four division headquarters. An officer could spend most of his career in the U.S. Army in Germany, and many did just that. The rest of the army called them the Imperial Army of the East, not a comment on American geopolitical designs but rather a comment on the self-importance of that force.

It was a good strategy, well-executed, and there was no war with the Soviet Union. But we fell into the mindset that we go to war with the army we have, which is wrong. We go to war with the army we can build.

The need to put in place the building blocks now for a future war-fighting army is an opportunity, not an obstacle. We can correct some of our current missteps. If it is our relatives and neighbors who go off to war, we are much more likely to go to war only for compelling causes. If a wide cross section of all Americans fight our wars when the need arises, all of America will go to war. A citizen soldier army means that our values are cross leveled between our citizens and our soldiers, to the benefit of both. The requirement to raise an army to go to war is a check on presidential adventuring and elective, preemptive wars.

The challenge is not just to have the best warfighting force possible. If that were the issue, we could simply update a World War II–sized military for today's America—twenty-seven million in uniform instead of the one plus million currently on active duty, 37 percent of our GDP to defense instead of 4 percent—and be done with it. That makes no more sense now than it did before the Civil War and the two world wars. The challenge is to have the best defense that is sustainable over time and that is consistent with our goals and values as a nation. That means putting in place now the pathways that will allow us to expand our forces when war comes.

Rebalancing our forces will require overcoming some lingering issues from the Vietnam War, one of the most divisive wars in our history. Vietnam drove a wedge between America and its army. The war there was fought by a conscripted force. These were the young men who could not get a college deferment, who could not wrangle a slot in the National Guard or a reserve unit, who could not work the system to avoid the war. Most of our soldiers—and many of our sailors, airmen, and marines—who were not actually drafted volunteered under the shadow of the draft. After four months of training, the army sent its soldiers as individuals, not as units, to Vietnam. There, perhaps one in ten joined a platoon of thirty others in the jungle or rice paddies for combat operations until they were killed, wounded severely enough to be shipped home, or until their year was over. The other nine went to support units in the rear where boredom, drugs, and racial strife were too often pervasive. The sense of isolation was nearly complete. In World War II, the troops spoke of America as home. In Vietnam, America was called back in the world. At the end of their year, they came back to the world as alone as they had gone, vilified by the very Americans they thought they had gone to war to protect.

Unlike America's previous wars, our elites did not go to war in Vietnam. It was more fashionable in some quarters to go to Canada than to volunteer for combat. When Winston Churchill resigned in disgrace as First Lord of the Admiralty after the debacle at the Dardanelles in World War I, he joined a regiment on the Western Front and fought as an infantry battalion commander.[5] In 1968, when Robert McNamara similarly resigned in disgrace in the face of a bankrupt and failed policy in Vietnam, no one entertained the idea that he might go join the people he had sent into combat. After he left the Pentagon, McNamara instead went to a lucrative and prestigious presidency of the World Bank. When Paul Wolfowitz, the deputy secretary of defense and a key advocate for the Iraq War, left the Pentagon as the war turned sour, he also became president of the World Bank. The expectation is no longer that all Americans fight our wars.

Vietnam also separated America's people from their government. A harbinger of that split occurred in 1965 in an unlikely place, the River Entrance to the Pentagon. The River Entrance is one of those tranquil spots in Washington that tourists seldom see. It is a parklike space, a well-kept enclave used for ceremonies to welcome visiting dignitaries to the Pentagon. A grass plaza overlooks the Potomac River. Across the river are the Washington Monument and the Jefferson Memorial, the Capitol Dome in the distance. The most warlike thing that happens in this pristine space is the boom of the ceremonial salute artillery used in full honors ceremonies.

The secretary of defense's office is on the third floor of the Pentagon overlooking the River Entrance. During Vietnam, McNamara was a favorite target of the anti-war activists. Among the most extreme—and to Americans most incomprehensible—forms of protest was the self-immolation of Buddhist monks in Vietnam.[6] Pictures of those grisly suicides in Saigon shocked America. In November 1965, an American anti-war protester set himself ablaze below the secretary's window at the Pentagon's River Entrance. Gruesome death, so commonplace in Vietnam, intruded the tranquility of the national capital.[7]

The break between Americans and their government was severe. In the Tet Vietnamese New Year celebration of 1968, the North Vietnamese and Viet Cong launched a countrywide offensive designed to expel the Americans and topple the American-sustained government of South Vietnam. In the days and weeks that followed, the most deadly combat of the entire Vietnam War took place. Casualties soared on both sides, but the Communist losses were many times those of the Americans and the South Vietnamese. The Viet Cong held none of the ground that they briefly occupied and their severe casualties crippled them as a fighting force for years. But the surprise and intensity of the attack, in stark contrast to the assurances of pending victory from Secretary of Defense McNamara and General William Westmoreland, gave the North Vietnamese a decisive psychological victory. The anti-war movement in America, already at fever pitch, spiraled to new levels. Riots and demonstrations spread.

At the height of the Tet offensive, Westmoreland engaged in a bit of bureaucratic gamesmanship of the sort that flourished in the McNamara years. At the likely urging of the chairman of the Joint Chiefs of Staff, Westmoreland asked for two hundred thousand additional troops.[8] That on top of the half million he already had. That in spite of the fact that he knew it would take six to twelve months to draft, train, and deploy those forces. And that in the midst of an enemy onslaught where even the American Embassy had been attacked by the Viet Cong.

In evaluating the request for troops, the Pentagon planners felt called upon to assess whether the army would have enough forces still in the United States to deal with the growing riots and anti-war demonstrations.[9] In simple terms, the army had to husband forces for use against the American people. That such planning was called for indicates how badly the government was split from its citizens regarding Vietnam. The purpose of the U.S. Army is to defend America in time of war, not to be used against Americans to enforce an unpopular war policy. Not since Lincoln sent troops just out of battle at Gettysburg to quell draft riots in New York had American military forces been so used.[10]

Vietnam distanced Americans from the American way of war. The cause for the war in Vietnam turned out to be less than compelling. Civilian and military leaders pursued a deeply flawed strategy. Conscripted forces fought the war. Our values were too often misplaced. All of America did not go to war. America's freedom was not, in fact, challenged.

All this is much clearer now than it was at the time. My first publication was an article in the journal of the Army War College.[11] I was a Special Forces major and, with more than a little trepidation, submitted an article to the effect that we lost the war in Vietnam because presidents and secretaries of defense and generals made mistakes and poor decisions. That article split the War College review panel sharply down the middle. Half of them wanted the article prominently published. Half thought it was not the kind of thing military officers should be saying and did not want it published at all. The go-for-it faction won and those views have since become commonplace.

The hardest part of writing the article was penning the phrase "lost the war."

In a pique over Vietnam, Congress passed the War Powers Resolution in 1973. That law requires presidents to notify Congress when they are sending military forces into combat, tell Congress how those forces are doing, and either follow the Constitution and obtain a declaration of war or bring the troops home.[12] In the years since its passage, a Washington two-step has been danced around the War Powers Resolution. The White House complies or does not while saying that it doesn't have to comply. Congress demands compliance while accepting whatever the White House does or does not send it. Presidents are given to saying that the nation is at war, against terrorism and in Iraq, but no one seriously considers the need for a declaration of war.

The gap between America and America going to war was widened by another Vietnam aftermath event, the end of the Cold War–era draft. There was much uncertainty at the time about an all-volunteer army. Old soldiers, as old soldiers will, bemoaned the loss of enforced patriotism that would no longer be visited upon succeeding generations. Government budgeteers worried about the cost. Social critics worried that there would be too many or too few minorities, too many or too few women in the future military.

What actually happened was that more motivated recruits joined our ranks. Discipline, a report card for the health of a command, improved dramatically. In the draft era, every army post had a stockade. After the draft ended, the stockades were closed. A soldier is unlikely to go AWOL from a volunteer force. There may be enlistment contract issues, but those are not stockade issues. The quality of the troops increased measurably and the quality of the troops' performance increased even more.

Our volunteer force was an important part of restoring the American military after Vietnam. But the draft had levied among Americans the responsibility of defending America. Imperfectly, certainly, but still a levy. Our current army is unquestionably capable but just as unquestionably less connected to the American public.

We need a different kind of army set within a different policy framework. There is no air valve in our current army where you can attach a pump and simply make our current force bigger. Army expansion is not a linear projection. Our current standing army can be expanded, but that expansion takes some understanding. And it requires thinking through now what we will do when war comes.

The idea is to take what works and raise new army formations when needed. Training standards are high in our current army, and they should remain high. A smaller, well-trained force will beat a poorly trained larger force. Our officer corps works. A good battalion commander in a small army can become a good general in a large army. Dwight Eisenhower went from lieutenant colonel and battalion command to lieutenant general and theater command in less than eighteen months in World War II.[13] Most good infantry soldiers in our current squads can become good squad leaders in an expanded army. The tactics and operational concepts we have now for our small army work just as well for a larger army. We can build strength upon strength: keep what works now and find ways ahead that recapture the fundamental sources of our past victories.

To do that, we must rebalance our army between standing forces and citizen soldiers. That is a foundation of the American way of war. We have abandoned that strength, to our loss.

CHAPTER 9:

The Next Pentagon

AMERICA'S MILITARY LEADERSHIP comes from the Pentagon. We can do better there in several ways: the next Pentagon should mandate an enforced joint approach across the full spectrum of military operations, should look to generals and admirals for hard-edged counsel, should increase the authority of the chairman of the Joint Chiefs of Staff, and should think more deeply.

Pentagon reform is not a new problem. The day the Japanese dropped their bombs on Pearl Harbor, the army was a moribund collection of branch fiefdoms. The chief of cavalry decided what was best for the cavalry, the chief of coast artillery for the coast artillery, and so on. The chiefs of the branches had worked their way up the promotion ladder by seniority. They each had supporting lobbies on Capitol Hill, and they stoutly defended their considerable prerogatives. As a result, the pre–Pearl Harbor U.S. Army was an often uncoordinated lurching of branch enthusiasms. More often, lack of enthusiasms.[1]

Miscues were routine. After World War I, there was a twenty-year debate over the value of the cavalry, as in horse cavalry, versus the value of tanks. The answer seems obvious now, but it apparently was not obvious at the time. Patton and Eisenhower, as captains and majors, were then the subject matter experts for armor and tried to make a case for a mechanized force. Eisenhower was curbed by infantry branch and Patton, being Patton, temporized on this career-threatening issue.[2] Cavalry branch got the better of the debate. The horses won.

George Marshall's first target after the Pearl Harbor attack was not the Japanese or the Germans, it was the army branch baronies. He reorganized the army into ground, air, and service commands.[3] Older officers were summarily retired. It took the president's signature to authorize the reorganization and a world war to get Congress on the sidelines.

The four service branches today are very much like the old army branch baronies that Marshall faced. They are chartered to be advocates for their role, doctrine, and equipment. They have Capitol Hill lobbies, tended faithfully by the contractors and their lobbyists, who support the services' equipment needs. The services defend their prerogatives with enthusiasm. Because the services make their own equipment decisions, the joint capabilities on which precision warfare rests are not a given. Compatibility issues are referred to a committee with the usual level of committee results: slow, cumbersome, with hit-and-miss performance.[4] Purposeful and coordinated movement toward a better joint warfight is not the default setting for Pentagon decision making. That limits our warfighting potential.

The most successful reform of the Pentagon since the building was constructed and opened in 1942 was the Goldwater-Nichols Act of 1986. It restructured how the Pentagon does business. The basic thrust of the Goldwater-Nichols Act was to take authority away from the services and give it to the chairman of the Joint Chiefs of Staff and the warfighting combatant commanders.

Goldwater-Nichols began when a serving chairman of the Joint Chiefs of Staff was willing to go before Congress and say that a creaking and fractious Pentagon needed a more joint approach to warfighting.[5] That revelation was made in a closed hearing, but "closed" in leak-plagued Washington is a relative term. The generals and admirals back across the Potomac River were appalled and then alarmed. They fought the move to a more joint Pentagon tooth and nail for years. Overwrought predictions were made that such reforms would imperil the security of the nation. Today, the Pentagon leadership will, almost to a person, sing the praises of the changes.

It is time to move to the next level of reform. The direction needed now became clear after a painful setback for American arms in the later years of the Carter presidency. The Shah of Iran, widely viewed in the Middle East as a creature of American imperialism, was deposed in 1979. In the paroxysm of revolution in Iran that followed, the American embassy in Tehran was seized and the embassy staff taken hostage. Their fate was uncertain: threats of trial and torture and execution were made and believed. An irresolute diplomacy gained little, although a fundamentalist state that made hostages of diplomats may not have been subject to diplomatic pressure in any event.

Planning for a military rescue began just days after the hostages were taken. It yielded an ambitious and complicated plan. Army Special Forces soldiers were to attack the embassy compound to free the hostages. To get there, they would fly on air force C-130 transport aircraft to an isolated desert landing strip deep inside Iran, a site that became known as Desert One. Navy helicopters piloted by marine pilots were to launch from an aircraft carrier in the Gulf of Oman and fly to Desert One. The helicopters would refuel and take the Special Forces assault team to a clandestine site outside Tehran and then fly to a separate location. The Special Forces soldiers would remain hidden for the day, move by truck into the city that night, and attack the embassy. Once the hostages were in hand, the helicopters were to fly into Tehran, land on a soccer field near the embassy compound and pick up the rescuers and the rescued. They would fly everyone to an Iranian airfield that was to have been attacked and secured by a second American force. Everyone would board C-141 transports and fly to safety.[6]

That sort of operation is enormously difficult. It requires land, sea, and air forces that train together, have compatible equipment, and are working from the same doctrine. Because the army, navy, air force, and marines all provided their own forces and equipment, joint mission training for the operation was incomplete, equipment compatibility issues remained unresolved, and the common tactics, techniques, and procedures that flow from joint doctrine and habitually training together fell short. Control of this complicated operation was given to a temporary task force set up for that purpose.

The mission came apart en route. The helicopters flying to Desert One developed mechanical problems: there were not enough of them still airworthy to complete the mission. The operation was aborted but in the confusion of refueling at Desert One to reverse course and fly home, a helicopter flew into a C-130, killing eight Americans. Days later, media coverage showed an Iranian mullah gleefully displaying the charred remains of our casualties.

If courage and resolve could have carried the day, the hostages would in fact have been rescued. The skill and commitment of the forces on the mission were not at issue. The things that came apart flowed from how the Pentagon did business. The sources of the mission failure were the lack of established joint command, doctrine, equipment, and training.

After many of the Desert One mistakes were repeated in the use of Special Operations forces in Grenada in 1983, a solution to the Pentagon way of doing its Special Operations business was found. The Cohen-Nunn Amendment to the Goldwater-Nichols Act mandated that the Pentagon establish a permanent joint headquarters for all Special Operations forces. That headquarters was given servicelike responsibilities, much to the consternation of the army, navy, and air force. All land, sea, and air Special Operations forces were permanently assigned to the new headquarters, which, importantly, had its own budget authority. Those forces trained together every day, bought compatible equipment, and wrote truly joint doctrine. The four-star commander of Special Operations Command had the authority to beat the rest of the bureaucracy into submission on Special Operations issues. Within that protected space, the mission capability of the assigned units soared.

Success in the Special Operations community has become routine. For Desert Storm, they were the glue that held much of the Coalition forces tactically together. After the September 11th terrorist attacks, Special Operations forces deployed to Afghanistan to help displace a fundamentalist and repressive régime. In combating terrorism in far flung parts of the world, Special Forces are the military option of choice.

The Pentagon, with some heavy-handed help from Congress, fixed its Special Operations problems. We need to take the same enforced joint approach across the full spectrum of military operations. While the need for joint operations on the battlefield is self-evident, the Pentagon policymaking processes that will produce joint capabilities are not in place and are, in fact, often actively resisted by the turf- and budget-defending services.

The day before his inauguration, John F. Kennedy and several close advisers visited the White House to meet with the outgoing president. Eisenhower was then seventy years old, and had been the five-star commander in Europe in World War II while Kennedy was a very junior navy lieutenant in the Pacific. Eisenhower's public persona was rambling, a touch befuddled, and comfortably middle class. Kennedy's image was youthful, vigorous, affluent, and stylish.

Kennedy had campaigned on the idea that he needed to get America moving again, a not very subtle suggestion that the elder Eisenhower had left America leaderless. Kennedy had also campaigned on an alleged missile gap, the suggestion that the Soviets had stolen a missile march on the United States while Eisenhower was asleep at the switch. There was no missile gap and, by the time they met, certainly Eisenhower (and probably Kennedy as well) knew there was no missile gap.[7] The meeting was cordial but perhaps a bit strained.

To Kennedy's surprise, Eisenhower told him that his new administration would face the imminent possibility of a war in Laos against Communist insurgents.[8] On the Saturday morning following his inauguration, Kennedy assembled his secretary of defense, secretary of state and key White House staffers to consider their military options in Southeast Asia. This early meeting set a pattern for how Kennedy would deal with military issues, an approach that distanced senior military officers from final defense decision making.

The people present at this Saturday meeting were demonstrably accomplished. Among their number were lawyers and academics from Harvard and MIT. They discussed counterinsurgency plans and detailed troop levels for the Army of the Republic of Vietnam. The only military officer in the room was a wildly out of channels air force brigadier general, Edwin Lansdale, who styled himself a counterinsurgency expert. No one in a uniform who had responsibility for military matters was present.[9]

That meeting proved to be typical of how Kennedy dealt with Vietnam. He did not often seek the counsel of senior military officers and did not give weight to the counsel he received.[10] After the debacle of the CIA-sponsored invasion of Cuba at the Bay of Pigs, Kennedy viewed himself as having been poorly served by the Joint Chiefs of Staff. To help fix what he saw as a problem, Kennedy recalled to active duty the retired General Maxwell Taylor.[11]

Taylor was very much in the Kennedy mold. He came back to active service from the presidency of the Lincoln Center for Performing Arts in New York. Taylor was an Airborne general with a distinguished war record, but a general of uncommon culture who, after retiring, had written a well-received book critiquing Eisenhower's dependence on nuclear weapons. While still army chief of staff, Taylor had opposed the Eisenhower New Look policy but was loyally circumspect. After retiring, Taylor offered a competing theory of flexible response, meaning that presidents ought to have something less cataclysmic than a nuclear strike among their military options. It was an obviously sensible position but was also an idea that could have been crafted with a vigorous president like Kennedy and a murky problem like Vietnam in mind.

After the Bay of Pigs, Taylor was installed in the White House, in uniform, as something called the "Military Representative of the

President." He was, in effect, a handler of the Joint Chiefs of Staff (JCS) housed in the White House to get Kennedy military counsel without having to deal with the real JCS. It was a thoroughly bad idea. When Taylor eventually moved over to the Pentagon to become the actual chairman of the JCS, the military representative position in the White House was thankfully never filled again.[12]

Under the civilianized defense decision making process he favored, Kennedy was unlikely to get the kind of bad news presidents need to get when making go-to-war decisions. America slipped into a war in Vietnam without one of the core requirements of the American way of war: a compelling cause. The South Vietnamese government that America would defend at such great cost measured its worth not in terms of the Vietnamese people but in terms of its closeness to the American aid that was flowing into Vietnam. The Kennedy and Johnson staffers, for all their erudition, seemed to have misplaced their understanding of the proper role of governments.

The last leader of South Vietnam with even a plausible claim to legitimacy was Ngo Dinh Diem. Diem and his brother Nhu, the head of South Vietnam's internal security forces, ruthlessly crushed even moderate opposition to the Diem regime. Anti-Diem sentiment spread when Nhu used U.S.-trained Vietnamese Special Forces to raid Buddhist pagodas and arrest religious leaders. The staffers in the Kennedy White House referred to the policy option of supporting the always difficult Diem and his tenuous claim to govern as "sink or swim with Ngo Dinh Diem."[13] They didn't swim. With explicit American consent and tacit American approval, Diem was deposed by a military coup in early November 1963.[14] He and his brother were killed by the plotters the day after the coup.[15] President Kennedy was assassinated later the same month.

The legitimacy issue of governing in Vietnam faded from importance ever more quickly. A series of revolving door military coups took place in Saigon. Each new Vietnamese general seizing power proved to be something less than a statesman. After yet another coup,

Maxwell Taylor, who had left the chairmanship of the Joint Chiefs of Staff to become America's ambassador to South Vietnam, articulated the "rock-bottom criterion . . . which asks only for a government to exist and to have the strength of voice able to ask for U.S. help."[16]

Vietnam became an American war, defined more by politics in Washington than by any compelling cause for war in Vietnam.

It is easy—too easy—to take cheap shots at the American leaders who were wrong about Vietnam and, in its turn, wrong about Iraq. The events of both were lived, and decisions made, prospectively. Judging the impact of those decisions is done retrospectively. Still, it is worth knowing what our leaders did and why they did it. That should make us better able to deal with the Vietnams and Iraqs in our future.

The key figure in the policymaking that took America to war in Vietnam was Robert McNamara; for Iraq, Donald Rumsfeld. McNamara and Rumsfeld took firm control of the Pentagon, increasing their authority at the expense of their generals and admirals. In the final analysis, civilian control of the military trumps both good and bad ideas from generals and admirals. An assertive, long-serving secretary of defense will eventually have his way. McNamara and Rumsfeld's increasing control of the Pentagon decreased the likelihood of policy dissent and rethinking just when policy changes on both wars were most needed.

Their policies were wrong. The government we were supporting in Vietnam had little and lessening legitimacy. The government we were supporting in Iraq came about more as a product of American policy than from popular support among the Iraqi people. The wars McNamara and Rumsfeld chose to fight could not be won the way they chose to fight them. The massive combat power we brought to bear did not address the central issue of political allegiance to an emerging government. Military success could avoid losing these wars but could not win them: winning or losing would be determined by events outside our control, perhaps outside our influence. Both

McNamara and Rumsfeld—and Lyndon Johnson and George Bush—deserved a general who knew that and who could convince them of that before their political capital and credibility with the American public were squandered.[17]

What exactly, with the benefit of hindsight, would we have wanted a general to do about the flawed Vietnam and Iraq policies as they were building? To have the professional acuity and breadth of vision to see the flaws in the strategy. And to have the strength of character to force that dissenting view on a president. Go-to-war decisions are an area where presidents should seek contentious counselors who press hard choices. Presidents can choose to take that advice or not, but the advice must be offered. On both Vietnam and Iraq, someone wearing stars should have been the forceful bearer of bad news to the president. That did not happen. The wars in Iraq and Vietnam are the kind of mistake we expect our generals and admirals to avoid.

The thing that the Pentagon most needs to be able to do well, it now does poorly: make decisions. A tactic that has been repeatedly tried for getting the Pentagon on track over the last half-century of reform has been to strengthen the authority of the secretary of defense. Ground has been gained that way since 1947 but the room for further improvement is limited. Short of issuing them field marshal's batons, secretaries of defense are already about as muscular as they can be made to be.

We need to carve out some additional authority and responsibility for our senior serving officer, the chairman of the Joint Chiefs of Staff. We should give the chairman JCS more authority on budget and major equipment matters, subject to review by the secretary of defense, the White House, and Congress. The chairman already has the responsibility to make final recommendations to the secretary on both strategy proposals and service budget submissions. That process is now done in secret.[18] The chairman should have more budget, force structure, and major equipment decision authority and his decisions should be a public part of our strategy development.

The immediate gains of giving the chairman greater authority are significant. Underfunded military operations do not unravel gracefully. Because the moving parts must fit together—the training and procurement and lift and communications—a modest mistake setting priorities anywhere in the process can have immodestly bad results when war comes. An F-22 without enough precision-guided munitions is of little value. The best tank in the world becomes second rate if its four crewmen haven't had enough time on a firing range. A great army or fleet or air component with a mediocre commander will most often turn in a mediocre performance. It is unrealistic to expect a civilian analyst in the office of the secretary of defense to understand all that. A JCS chairman knows it at a glance.

A strengthened chairman will be a better help to presidents and secretaries of defense as they wrestle with the always unwieldy Pentagon. The generals and admirals who run the services will do what they think is best for their service. Secretaries of defense don't know, and can't be expected to know, enough about the details of running each branch of the military or a war to direct their flag officers in detail. It is a mistake to try. Secretaries can't run the Pentagon directly, but chairmen of the Joints Chiefs of Staff can. Secretaries need to run chairmen.

The army, navy, air force, and marines are force providers and they are very good at that mission. We need to keep the services at their force providing tasks and stay out of their way. The system comes off the rails when the services use their clout to shape policy decisions to protect their service turf. If they tilt a policy decision, and they tilt as hard as they can as often as they can, they are doing the job we gave them. Most army generals are convinced that what is good for the army is good for America. As are air force generals about the air force, navy admirals about the navy, and marine generals about the marines. In that rare instance where what is good for America is not inescapably good for one's service, chances are slim that the obvious solution is to fund something for another service.

We are already retooling our flag officer mindset, moving from a service-centric senior officer culture to a more joint warfighting outlook. Promotion to flag rank now requires joint experience, and our growing corps of joint warfighters is an asset that George Marshall never had. The Goldwater-Nichols Pentagon reform legislation made substantial progress across the board and more progress along the same path is required. A chairman with increased authority will help.

Here is how that should work.

The army has two light infantry divisions. Light infantry soldiers have no tanks or infantry fighting vehicles. They are organized, equipped and trained for terrain where tanks generally don't want to go: mountains, cities and jungles. They have a rifle, a radio to call for help and an attitude. Light fighters like to say that when all else fails, they can crawl out of their fighting position and kill someone with their bare hands. That is, in fact, true.

The basic unit of the Marine Corps is light infantry. They can come across a defended beach, no mean feat. Often in today's environment, the marines come ashore by helicopter. Just like the army does. Once on the ground, the marines fight like any other light infantrymen but with less long-term sustainment capability.

The obvious question is: why do we maintain largely duplicative capabilities in both the army and the marines? The not so obvious answer lies in Pentagon and Washington politics. If a secretary of defense tried to eliminate the army light infantry divisions, the Congressional delegations where those divisions are based would lay siege to the Pentagon. The budget would be held hostage. If all else failed, an individual senator might simply stop all promotions to general officer until the light division in his state was safe. If a secretary of defense tried to cut the marines, there would be an even greater response from Congress and an even greater hue and cry from the public. There is a long-standing witticism in the Pentagon that if they added an additional member to a marine infantry squad, he would be a cameraman. The marines are a great fighting force and an equally adept public relations force.

What is a secretary of defense to do? If cuts must be made, or plus-ups funded, the secretary should have his chairman, a four-star uniformed officer, propose the changes on the merits. If either cuts or increases are the right thing to do, any chairman will do it. If either is the wrong thing to do, a secretary of defense needs to hear that early and clearly. Congressmen will, without hesitation, substitute their political judgment for a secretary's. They are less likely to substitute their military judgment for a chairman's.

One of the Cold War skills that our current Pentagon process still uses is counting things: tanks and planes and ships and army formations. That was the right approach when mass, the sum of all those things being counted, determined what happened on the battlefield. But our current precision joint warfight and our engagement missions and counter-terrorist operations require a different Pentagon skill: we need to be able to assess capabilities and then combine those capabilities, deploy them, and direct them with the same fidelity we previously achieved for counting things. Letting a chairman have greater authority on budget and equipment issues injects the expertise that will help us move from counting things to assessing and funding capabilities, and it does so early in the process.

A reformed Pentagon can also be bolder on time frames. What we are calling army transformation is scheduled to take thirty-two years. At base, the change is to go from a seventy-ton vehicle—which, by the way, has crept up to seventy-five tons since the Cold War ended—to a twenty-ton vehicle and adjusting the technology and the support tail involved. In World War I, Pershing held off the demands to feed American units piecemeal into the French and British armies already in the trenches. One of the more telling arguments he faced was that it would take field army, corps, and division staff officers to fight the U.S. Army Pershing was building. Since our army had no unit larger than a regiment before it got to France, staff officer expertise was a legitimate issue. Told by the French and British that it would take thirty years to build the general staff needed, Pershing scoffed, "It never took America thirty years to do anything."[19] Perhaps not in Pershing's army. Certainly it does in our army today.

Pershing's assured confidence remained the way of things through World War II. The P-51 fighter escort, probably the best fighter fielded by any nation during the war and arguably the key operational aircraft of any type, was designed and built in ninety days.[20] Our current best fighter, the F-22, became operational twenty-five years after the first design requirements documents were completed in 1982. This snail's pace of change in the military is a self-inflicted wound. We have slipped into decisions by committee in a zero-defect environment. The P-51 was initially a failure; it took bolting a British engine onto the American-built plane to bring it to life. Today, that kind of misstep would give us a media firestorm, Congressional hearings, and no airplane.

The next Pentagon should also think more deeply. Budgets, equipment, and technology matter but the fundamentals of the American way of war matter much more. Senior military officers cannot fix the shortfalls in civilian policymaking: that is the responsibility of civilians. But military officers can bring enduring values to the process.

Values matter. During the American Revolution, the Continental Congress often failed to pay its soldiers. At the close of the Revolution, Congress was no better at that than they had been during the war. George Washington's officers, in cabal, resolved to take by force from Congress what they were admittedly owed. The theory was that any soldier with a musket could have the better of an argument with any politician who lacked one.[21] Congress decamped from Philadelphia for Princeton, then to Annapolis, fleeing not from the British but from their own army.[22] Washington addressed his officers and dissuaded them. Challenging the civilian government they had fought so hard to bring to life would, in Washington's phrase, tarnish both the glory of their victory and the reputation of their army. Because he was Washington, because he was who he was to his army, Washington had his way.[23] His belief that civilians should control the military passed into the fabric of our officer corps. The years since have only strengthened that belief. Soldiers still have muskets and politicians still do not: the deeply ingrained value of civilian control of the military is an asset of inestimable value.

Robert E. Lee and Ulysses S. Grant added to our senior officer value set. Their generalship converged for the last time at an important event and place, at Appomattox in April 1865. They ended the war, these two soldiers, on a basis that was critical in reuniting the two warring halves of America. Facing the necessity of surrender, Lee did not follow the Confederate President's call to dissolve his army into the rural reaches of the South and to wage a protracted and divisive guerrilla war against the conquering army of the North.[24] Lee refused to do that on the same basis as his decision to join the Confederacy in the first place: personal honor. The partisan warfare that had plagued the Civil War thus far had been armies fighting civilians and civilians fighting armies. That was beyond the bounds of war as Lee knew war. At Appomattox, the Confederate commander was looking for a way to end the conflict, not prolong it.[25]

Grant was as well. Bloody civil wars usually end in more bloodshed, not in reconciliation. At Lincoln's urging and by his own inclination, Grant offered Lee a generous and conciliatory peace. There were to be no drumhead courts martial, no summary executions. Lee's soldiers were not to be made prisoners, his officers were not to be tried as traitors. They were allowed to go home and resume their lives as if no war had occurred, conditioned only on Lee's word and their word that they would not again take up arms against the government.[26]

The terms of surrender offered by Grant to Lee's army became the basis for the surrender of the other Confederate armies still in the field and, in fact, became the basis on which the war ended. It was a decision reached by two generals who had fought each other to the death. Grant and Lee rose above their respective causes. Restoring the Confederates' freedom would restore the Union and would begin healing the wounds of the war.

Core values also came into play as the army withdrew from Vietnam. The army was in dire straits: drug use was widespread, race relations army-wide were in deadly uproar, indiscipline was rampant. The task of rebuilding the army fell first to Creighton Abrams, the commander in Vietnam for the last five years of the war and then army chief of staff. When Abrams set about restoring the U.S. Army, he made a bold change. Abrams understood that the army had bled itself dry in a long war in the jungles of Vietnam, a war fought without the support of the American people and, ultimately, for little purpose. He resolved to keep that from happening again. How he did it showed a deep understanding of the bond between America and its army.

Abrams put in place what he called the Total Force policy. That meant, quite simply, that he mixed together the active army, the army reserve, and the army National Guard so that America could not go to war without a large call-up of reserve soldiers. Abrams had seen President Johnson go to war in Vietnam without the reserve call-up that had been a part of every war plan in the Pentagon. Despite the unanimous advice of his senior military officers, Johnson refused to call up the reserves for the war in Vietnam. The president did not call up the reserves and did not take the nation to a war footing because the politics of it were wrong. He was playing down America's commitment to a war in Vietnam, purposefully disguising the war's costs in people and money. The White House staff viewed calling up the reserves as the political sound barrier.[27] They didn't have the good judgment to break through that barrier. Johnson succeeded at this sleight of hand but at terrible cost. When the bills from Vietnam came due, and they inevitably did come due, the American people had little commitment to a war in Vietnam.

To prevent that from happening again, Abrams structured his Total Force. A National Guard artillery battalion would support an active-duty armor brigade whose tanks were kept running by an army reserve maintenance company. That meant that a president could not send the army to war without calling up the Guard and reserve, and he had to make a case for war to the public and Congress. Abrams was tying the hands of future presidents. It was heroically insubordinate, completely within the rules, and done for all the right reasons. At the time, no one paid a great deal of attention to this bit of army organizational minutiae. When the build-up for Desert Storm began in 1990, the civilian leadership in the Pentagon had to confront the fact that they could not deploy to the Persian Gulf without a very large reserve call-up.

The White House and Pentagon leadership during Desert Storm was very much a part of the Vietnam generation. The mistakes and misjudgments of Vietnam still weighed heavily on American policy-making. The Pentagon ordered the reserve call-up and the leadership hunkered down, half-expecting demonstrations and anti-war marches.[28] There were marches, many of them, but they were parades and send-offs for the hometown reservists and Guardsmen. The outpouring of support for the soldiers going off to war proved to be a very short step from support for the war itself. The reserve call-up for Desert Storm required facing the cost of a war in the Persian Gulf, a step that Lyndon Johnson had purposefully avoided for Vietnam. It was a hurdle along the path to war, knowingly put in place by a farsighted soldier.

These successes came from individual officers acting from their core beliefs. Our senior officers in the Pentagon today can do that as well as any of their predecessors, but they have to be allowed to do it. Secretaries of defense and presidents select senior officers. If their criteria for selection emphasizes administration-friendly views, they are less likely to get the pointed counsel they need. They leave an enormous American asset—the core values of our senior officers—out of the mix.

America's approach to civil/military matters has worked in the past. The introduction of a general staff organization in 1903 let America's senior officers and presidents direct the large, industrial-based wars of the twentieth century. The Cold War strategy of containment and deterrence confronting the Soviet Union spanned decades and successive presidential administrations and was a singular success. The post–Cold War sea change of precision warfare came from disparate parts of the Pentagon seeking technology fixes to their tactical problems. Defense and strategy decisions can be made well and can succeed.

To do that, our civilian leaders need to hold fewer committee meetings and instead ask their senior generals and admirals what America's next defense strategy should be. The current strategy update every four years has become a bureaucratic contest between civilians and generals over missions and budgets.[29] Even that unproductive effort is in place only because Congress mandates it. Truckloads of paper are produced, but insights seldom survive the process. The Pentagon can and should do significantly better.

The Pentagon is operating under fatally flawed rules. Korea, Vietnam, and the Iraq War represent a retreat from the American way of war. Congress no longer exercises its clear constitutional mandate to declare war on behalf of the American people. Presidents now send standing forces off to war, and the time-proven requirement that citizens become soldiers to fight the nation's wars has fallen by the way. Wars are waged for less than compelling causes, and victory or defeat has become a media determination. It is small wonder that, under these new rules, victory has eluded us.

There is a phrase that will send Pentagon generals and admirals into apoplexy. That phrase is "surplus readiness." The idea is that we are wasting money by being too ready to go to war. We are, and it is surprisingly easy to do.

All units, active and reserve, train to the same standard for deployment to war. They will fight their battles using the same doctrine. All require some period of time to get ready. Active units range from very little time required (for example, just days for the ready brigade of the 82nd Airborne Division) to months for a heavy unit coming out of an engagement mission like Bosnia or a security mission in Iraq. Reserve components range from days for some early deployers to months for heavy combat brigades.

Our war plans tell us when each unit needs to arrive in theater, precisely what day, where, and with what equipment. Our finite lift assets give us a specific schedule of when we can move units. Not when we want to, when we *can*. That tells us how much time we have for individual units, both active and reserve, to gather up their people and equipment, complete their training, and move to seaports and airfields. We go to war on a lift-driven schedule.

The challenge is to synchronize the war-planned mission requirements with the lift available and with the predeployment readiness of the units. The fever pitch of go-to-war levels of readiness wear out people, equipment, and budgets. Tiered readiness is an accepted part of the plan: the reason the 82nd has a rotating ready brigade is that keeping even one of its brigades at a hair-trigger alert status is a challenge. There is no virtue in maintaining difficult and perishable warfighting skills all day, every day if a unit is going to have a lift-mandated delay before it deploys. For a few units, that fever pitch level is required; for most of our force, that is surplus readiness.

Compare two armor brigades, one on active duty and the other in the National Guard. Subject to the normal fielding mismatches, both have the same equipment, even if often of a different vintage. Both have the same number of people, the identical organization, and train to the same standard for deployment to war. Their officers and noncommissioned officers receive the same training to qualify for their jobs and to be considered for promotion. The active-duty unit will have completed more—but not all—of its specific training tasks prior to deployment and will still need at least thirty days to get ready. The Guard brigade will have to complete some—but not all—of its training tasks, by design, after mobilization and will be ready to deploy at the same standard as the active-duty unit in ninety days.

Because we have a lift-mandated—and twice recently demonstrated—five- to six-month go-to-war schedule, we have the option of using those Guard brigades for much of the warfight. To do so frees more active-duty units to perform the interwar missions that decrease the likelihood of war in the first place. And to do so moves us back toward our Constitution and the basic design of how our government is supposed to make go-to-war decisions.

A hot button issue of this closed-door wrangling within the Pentagon is how much it costs to keep a unit on active duty and how much it costs to keep the same kind of unit in the reserve components, which will deploy at the same training standard. Because it relates to force structure, budget, and rank structure, that cost difference is among the most contested numbers in the Pentagon. This argument is pure testosterone.

It is, in truth, a hard number to pin down. How do you apportion equipment costs of second- and third-generation equipment cascaded down to the reserves? What portion of the institutional costs—the schools and infrastructure and administrative systems—should you attribute to the Guard and reserve? In the normal Pentagon way of things, whether you want the number to be big or small determines what numbers are assigned where. The direct operating costs can be tallied with some clarity. Of the current pay and allowances that do not go to retired pay, 10 percent goes to the half of the army that is in the Guard and reserve and 90 percent goes to the half of the army that is on active duty. Funding for operations and maintenance also goes 10 percent to the army reserve components, 90 percent to the active force.[30] That is the budgeted funding for the Guard and reserve in reserve status: if they are called to active duty, they cost as much as any active-duty soldier.

One unhelpful turf battle that we are putting behind us is the long-standing antipathy and competition between our active-duty and reserve components. Going to war together—first Desert Storm and then Iraq—will do that. Not going to war together, as happened in Vietnam, divides them. Important lessons have been learned. Sharing the mission burden is good. Sharing people is better. Having one standard, a high standard, is better still. With lift-driven train-up times known, we can move to a better model for the use of our active and reserve components, something smarter than the "give me the mission, give me the money" approach.

Much of our active-duty force should be used, as it has always been used and is being used now, for the military missions that arise between wars. Today, that is a full workload of engagement and smaller-scale contingencies and counter-terrorism missions. We are trying to keep those same active-duty forces as our primary warfighting force for conventional wars, as we did for the Cold War, and that is not working. There is no ignominy in using the full-time force for the full-time mission and the full-time mission has changed. Where once the full-time mission was to be ready for Cold War combat at any time, the full-time mission is now engagements and preventing wars before they happen.

Our failure to think beyond our Cold War requirement of going to war in a matter of hours with an active-duty force has come back to haunt our defense policymaking. The Constitution crafted at Philadelphia sought to make the decision to go to war harder, not easier, and it is too easy now for presidents and the Pentagon to send standing military forces off to war. The political hurdles are much higher in sending citizen soldiers, the current reserve components and potential national service soldiers. The standing military has fewer constituencies, there are no employers and fewer communities to answer to. Lyndon Johnson drove his Vietnam policy through that loophole. Centering our conventional warfighting capability on our citizen soldiers, as we have for our entire history save for the Cold

War, makes it harder to go to war and helps reestablish the critical link between America and America at war.

Our full-time military should concentrate on the full-time between war missions, maintaining training standards, and growing senior leaders to command citizen soldiers armies in time of war. Our current reserve components can be a bigger part of our current warfight force and a bridge to a larger citizen soldier army.

The Iraq War practice of embedding media reporters and camera crews with our maneuver units—a secretary of defense and White House decision—is a double-edged sword.[31] The military news from the combat phase of the war was always going to be good news. What happens in a future war when the news will be bad and when that news will give a tactical advantage to our enemies? The United States spends billions of dollars each year to be able to locate and track enemy units. Are we to offer real-time intelligence to our adversaries for the price of a used television set? If there is any doubt of the intelligence value of such information, ask our own intelligence analysts if they would like our enemies to broadcast around the clock with embedded reporters.

There is a tactical element to this media business, even in what passes for peacetime. Imagine yourself as an American naval officer in command of a destroyer coming into a port in the Middle East to refuel. You are on the bridge. In addition to being a very busy sailor just then, here are the things that might be in the back of your mind.

You know the USS *Stark* lost thirty-seven sailors to a missile hit in the Persian Gulf when the captain decided not to shoot at an approaching aircraft. He was disciplined. The USS *Vincennes* shot down an Iranian airliner by mistake, killing 290 civilians. The *Vincennes* captain did shoot and he was allowed to retire two years after the incident. The captain of the American submarine USS *Greeneville* was forced to resign when he accidentally sank the

Japanese school vessel *Ehime Maru*. The USS *Cole* lost seventeen sailors in Aden in precisely the circumstances you are taking your ship into.

Now imagine that a Zodiac boat just like the one that blew up the *Cole* starts speeding toward you. Do you shoot? Probably. Good choice.

Now imagine a Greenpeace banner on the front of the boat. They do that routinely. And add a media helicopter filming the whole thing. Now do you shoot? First you calculate the chances that a terrorist would be smart enough to hide behind a Greenpeace banner. Probably. Then you calculate what will happen if you are wrong and blow away some protesters, all of which will be live on television and the internet.

Do you shoot?

Much of what needs to be fixed in the Pentagon will have to be fixed from outside the Pentagon. The things that brought victory in our past are not now on the Pentagon agenda. Left to their own devices, the Pentagon leadership will focus on how to have the best force for the short-term missions rather than how to have the best force for the next major war. These are different puzzles with different pieces and we have to solve both puzzles at the same time. The role of citizen soldiers in our past victories is obvious, but resources and time and energy put to that long-term need will come at the expense of short-term combat readiness, force structure, or equipment. The essential need to take all of America to war when war comes and the power of going to war to defend America's freedom are concerns that rest well outside the Pentagon. Some of these issues will be addressed in the White House, some on Capitol Hill, but most must ultimately be resolved by our citizens. We get the government and the Pentagon we demand. We as citizens have set our expectations too low and have accepted too poor a performance.

CHAPTER 10:

Global Power

At the end of World War II, much of Europe lay in ruin. Six years of war there had killed tens of millions of people. More were injured, homeless, hungry. Bridges were destroyed, many roads were impassable. Across the continent, buildings and factories were shattered or abandoned. Of the factories that remained intact, many produced only war material, about the only thing in Europe that was not in short supply.

Farmers quit farming. There was little equipment to farm with, no way to get their goods to market, in fact, there was hardly a market to get them to. The currency to be had was suspect. Cigarettes and stockings were, in some places, a more reliable medium of exchange than official currencies. Had there been a passable currency, there was little to buy. Fuel stocks were dwindling because miners were not mining. Again, no equipment, no transport, no reliable market.[1] The manicured and trimmed trees of the Tiergarten in Berlin, the capital of a nation that cultivated trees to the level of a national fetish, were cut for firewood.

The less visible things of Europe were also destroyed. The banking and insurance systems had collapsed. Health care was limited and that which survived was overwhelmed with the shattered victims of the long years of war. The severe winter of 1947 stunned Europe.

In Britain, snow paralyzed the nation. Food and fuel became even harder to find.[2] And that was in England, which had so recently been the seat of Empire and wealth. In England, which had been among the victors in the war.

To the East, the Soviet menace loomed. Countries were pulled by force or the threat of force into the Soviet orbit: Poland, Lithuania, Estonia, Latvia, Hungary, Czechoslovakia, Romania, Bulgaria, and the Balkans. Communist parties in Italy and France were growing. The continent-wide devastation made the rest of Europe ripe for further Soviet encroachment.

Two men, both aging and both leaders in the war just won, offered an answer. Winston Churchill was thought to be past his time and was ousted as prime minister by Britain's voters at the moment of victory. His genius had been desperately needed in the darkest days of the war, but it seemed he would not be needed at all for the peace. In an infrequent moment of modesty, Churchill once disclaimed credit for the indomitable British stand against Hitler: "It was the nation and the race dwelling all round the world that had the lion's heart; I had the luck to be called upon to give the roar."[3]

There was another roar left in Churchill. He gave it in an unlikely setting, at a small college in Fulton, Missouri. He was there because President Harry Truman asked him to be.[4] More, Churchill was there because he had a speech to give and sought a prominent podium from which to give it. Truman offered the podium, Churchill made it prominent by standing to it. John Kennedy, himself no stranger to eloquence, later described Churchill in World War II as having "mobilized the English language and sent it into battle."[5] Churchill was ready to do that again.

In the metered Churchillian delivery, he said: "From Stettin in the Baltic to Trieste in the Adriatic, an Iron Curtain has descended across the continent."[6] Tyranny, dark and hidden, held sway on the other side of that curtain. Freedom dwelt only in the West, only in the victorious nations that now, save the United States, lay prostrate in the path of

Soviet aggression. Churchill's speech was a clarion call to action but one that was not well received at the time.[7]

One person who did heed Churchill's call was Secretary of State George Marshall, and he did so in a speech at the Harvard alumni luncheon on commencement day in 1947. Marshall painted a picture of a destitute Europe. He recounted the shortages of fuel, food, and the other essentials of life. A crisis was approaching quickly. Most needed were resources, cooperation, and leadership. Failing that, the victory of the war won at such great cost could be lost. America must step forward.[8]

The mechanics of what came to be called the Marshall Plan were straightforward. The United States made loans and grants to the countries of Europe that were left shattered by the war. The way the authors of the Marshall Plan went about it, however, showed a perceptive grasp of how to help. Save for some early emergency food shipments, the Marshall Plan was by and large not a relief effort but an economic recovery effort. Instead of just sending food, the Americans sent tractors so that European farmers could get back in production, sent machine tools so that factories could reopen.[9] The Marshall Plan was the critical margin for success in restarting the European economy.

It was a big program. The $17 billion spent over the years of the Marshall Plan, something on the order of $153 billion in today's dollars, was a significant commitment.[10] Many of America's most able men and women entered government service, a smaller version of the rush to get into uniform after Pearl Harbor, and for many of the same reasons. The Marshall Plan was viewed as, and in fact was, a matter of national defense. It used America's soft power assets—our economy, ideals, and a focused foreign policy—toward a national security goal.

The Marshall Plan rested on America's core strengths. The Cold War was, at base, a standoff between freely elected governments in the United States and Western Europe and an authoritarian regime in the Soviet Union. The West's strategy of containment and deterrence prevented war, but our Cold War success came only when the captive nations of the Soviet Union were no longer willing to accept their captive status. What won for the West was the idea of freedom, Jefferson's precept that people are by right free, and the robust economies that such freedom allows.

America is a global power with global interests. The best explanation of how America came to our current position of influence is that freedom is a compelling idea. America's current strength as a world power had its origins in a different era: the fashioning of the American form of self-government.

What passed for a federal government during the American Revolution was the Continental Congress. Each colony, some with more enthusiasm and some with less, sent representatives to meet and collectively decide the course of the colonists' war. One of their early decisions was one of their most important, although that was little recognized at the time. In the late spring of 1776, the Continental Congress, assembled in Philadelphia, resolved to publish a treatise to justify to the colonies and to the world the war they had already begun. To do that, they turned to Thomas Jefferson, a young and gifted delegate from Virginia. Jefferson gave voice to the events at Lexington and Concord and wrote a Declaration of Independence. His purpose was to explain a rebellion but, in the end, Jefferson's draft became an expression of why there was an America and what America might become.

A man of the Enlightenment era, Jefferson believed deeply that every mind must be free to follow its own inquiry, every person their own destiny. That sort of individual freedom would allow the America that Jefferson envisioned to become a meritocracy of knowledge and talent. The role of government was properly to protect its citizens' freedom to learn, to strive, and to seek a better life. Things that might threaten such freedom—the trappings of monarchy and clergy, standing armies of regular forces, the posturing of foreign powers, the taxes of a British parliament—had no place in Jefferson's vision. His thinking was so in tune with his country that if America was right, Jefferson was right. If America was wrong, Jefferson was wrong.[11]

Jefferson's talent was in both understanding these principles of liberty and in being able to write of them with clarity. Jefferson captured the thinking of his colleagues and crafted both a powerful case for a revolution and a compelling vision of America. A nation based on the freedom of all men, one with a government expressly subject to the needs and will of the governed. A nation of informed and self-reliant citizens, free to go where and as far as their abilities might carry them. Nothing like that existed then, but Jefferson and the others believed that it could.

The inherent sense of Jefferson's and his colleagues' thinking has worked, Jefferson's prescience confirmed when he used the phrase "contagion of liberty."[12] When the American colonists declared their independence, the prevailing form of government in the world was monarchy.[13] The thinking of Jefferson, Madison, and Washington and the acts of the colonists in battle were truly a revolution. Their cause had every likelihood of failing, its leaders every chance of being executed as traitors. But it did not fail, they were not executed, and two centuries and more later, the ideas of freedom that drove the American Revolution have shaped what America is and what it might yet become. The best description of Jefferson's continuing influence on America is the description of his continuing influence on the school he founded, the University of Virginia, and the campus of which he designed: it is as if Mr. Jefferson is in the next room.[14]

America is not a world power because it has a strong military. If that were possible, there would still be a Soviet Union. America is a world power because of its commitment to freedom. The world is a different place because there is a United States in it. That a nation can succeed on the basis of freedom is a beacon for other people who would be free and a warning to those who would deny them their liberty.

America must now chart a course in a fundamentally shifting international environment. Some of the shifts and swirls in the national security mix at the beginning of the twenty-first century come from the decline and demise of colonialism in the twentieth century.[15] When Theodore Roosevelt was president and the European colonial powers held sway, it was taken for granted that the affairs of less-developed countries could and should be ordered by more-developed nations. That meant that Europe and America directed much of the events in Africa and Asia. In poetic moments, the idea of colonialism passed from entitlement to obligation, hence Kipling's phrase of "the White Man's burden."

All of that, of course, was nonsense. As the twentieth century progressed, colonialism began to collapse under its own weight. World War II accelerated its end: a global war fought and won to ensure freedom for some nations eventually had to come to stand for freedom for all nations. Freedom is an idea that resists limits.

The world without colonialism would be less ordered. The onset of that disorder was delayed when the discipline of the Cold War replaced the previous colonial structure. Nations either chose a Cold War side or were chosen by a side, and both the United States and the Soviet Union kept a tight grip on their allies and dependencies. Nations not on either side still defined themselves by the Cold War division: they were nonaligned. Cold War rigor masked the potential for a post-colonial shift toward disorder among nations.

The sudden end of the Cold War ripped that mask away. Nations now choose their own course and their choices are determined by culture and self-interest. Islamic nations tend to group themselves by common identity and common interests. Asian nations are finding that their relationship to China is more important than their relationship to the former colonial powers and former Cold War ideologies. The Soviet Union has passed from the scene but Russia remains a regional force, is rearming militarily, and is still a nuclear power. Japan's reach is economic rather than cultural, but is significant.

India's influence is growing as the world's economy becomes less defined by national borders.[16] Latin America is more inwardly looking than expansionist, but is still becoming more culture conscious.[17] Writ large, these cultures become civilizations and they are civilizations in constant competition and occasional conflict.

Even what we used to confidently call the West—Europe and America—are going their separate ways.[18] Europe has become an economically intertwined European Union, a development that has lessened the likelihood of yet another war among European nations but has also encouraged a competition with the United States. America remains skeptical of supranational organizations and places its confidence in American diplomacy backed by American military power. The strengths that made America the winning superpower—its economy, its technology, and its sponsorship of democratic governments—have continued.

America's best course in the future will be its most consistent course from its past: defend our freedom when challenged and offer help to other nations as we can. America's military power is the result of our freedom, not the source of it. The values and ideals that underlie our freedom are more powerful than our tanks and ships and planes.

America has truly not garrisoned the world but, in what looks to be an act of unbecoming pride, the Pentagon has divided the world into military regions. There is a European Command with ninety-four countries in it. Pacific Command has fewer countries, more people, and a lot more water. There are two regions where war seems most likely: Korea and Southwest Asia. A less hostile geographic command is Southern Command, which covers Central and South America. There is an Africa Command that has more civilians in its headquarters and fewer troops on its troop list than is the norm. The North American Air Defense Command added the name Northern

Command to its title and added homeland defense to its mission after the September 11th attacks.

The military strength that the United States brings to bear can be more subtle than just blowing things up. That is clear in the role of the combatant commanders who oversee U.S. military forces in their regions. These four-star generals and admirals had traditionally been called commanders-in-chief, or CINCs. That title was acceptable, in some cases, for fifty years, but in a bit of Pentagon one-upmanship between Secretary of Defense Rumsfeld and his four-stars, the CINCs title was downgraded to combatant commanders.

By any name, they are an asset that goes well beyond warfighting. In Southern Command, the threat of conventional war against the sovereign territory of the United States is happily remote. Accordingly, the missions there have gravitated into other areas. A favorite measure of how well the theater commander in SOUTHCOM is doing is how well democracy in Central and South America is doing.

In the late 1970s, democracy in SOUTHCOM was not doing well. Most of the countries in the region were under some form of military dictatorship. By the late 1990s, almost all were democracies. Many were fledgling democracies, admittedly, but the trend was good. The health of those democracies, on which SOUTHCOM commanders spend much time, attention, and money, improved dramatically. It all made for a great series of before and after color-coded maps.

Coming upon this unawares, one might ask the very reasonable question: why is the military in the business of promoting democracy in Latin America and isn't that really a State Department job? Those issues, at least, are often raised by the State Department. The answer is that America and its military can do things other than just go to war. One of the most consistent threats to democracy in the countries in SOUTHCOM are the militaries in those countries. The generals in those militaries are much more likely to listen to SOUTHCOM's commander than they are to the State Department.

Such mentoring is not casual. The military leaders of the former Soviet states were assiduously courted by European Command as the Berlin Wall came down. These former Soviet satellite nations went from training for war against NATO to seeking NATO membership. Our military effort to support democracy around the world is planned, budgeted, and coordinated, year in and year out. What we are doing is using the power of our ideals and values—Jefferson's contagion of liberty—to promote peace and stability in a tumultuous world. Our values become tactical. Freedom can be as compelling a cause for peace as defending freedom is for war.

Roles other than warfighting take our combatant commanders into troubled waters. A commander of American and NATO forces in Europe was branded a war criminal for the air campaign in Kosovo by Serb leaders, who were terrorizing and making refugees of hundreds of thousands of non-Serb Kosovars. The Serbian accusations were widely reported in the media. The prosecutors of the UN International Tribunal for the former Yugoslavia at the Hague felt called upon to announce that they had considered whether to indict the American NATO commander for war crimes and had decided against it.[19]

War crimes are easy to talk about but difficult to codify. Standards and perspectives shift. Henry Kissinger directed the American withdrawal of forces from Vietnam too slowly for the anti-war movement and was branded a war criminal. Another group thought he was more on pace and awarded him a Nobel Peace Prize. Jane Fonda, forever to be known as Hanoi Jane to Vietnam veterans, either shamefully did the same things for which Tokyo Rose was convicted of treason and sent to prison after World War II or heroically gave voice in opposition to an unjust war.[20] Take your choice. Which you choose will probably depend less on what Kissinger and Fonda did and more on how you view the war in Vietnam.

The theater commanders get singled out as easy targets, but the real issue is America's position in the post–Cold War era. America has a unique role and must claim a unique status. We were late getting into

Bosnia and a quarter million people died. When the Serb Army was killing ethnic Albanian civilians in Kosovo, it was a good thing for the United States to deploy forces to stop the killing. We should have been in Rwanda but simply missed the boat. We should have been in Darfur but were fully focused on Iraq. Only America has the military forces to lead such an effort. Going into a politically charged conflict, there will inevitably be a media-driven duel of allegations and counter-allegations. Ideologically motivated prosecutors of transnational bodies will follow their own political agenda or the whims of a frenzied press. That is Third World politics more than studied justice.

If America is to be a world leader for peace and stability, we must lead and hold ourselves accountable to the fundamentals of our own values and ideals. How America is viewed by the rest of the world is important, but our own laws and judgment on such matters are more useful than the opinion of a UN functionary or a transnational commission prosecutor from Tobago.

America's military power has limits. There are some things that our military cannot do, try as we might or wish as we might. Saving failed states is one of them.

In Somalia in 1969, there was a coup that brought a dictator named Siad Barre to power. Barre aligned himself with the Soviet Union and nationalized what little Somali industry there was. That had the entirely predictable effect of strangling the already short of breath Somali economy. An interminable civil war broke out between Barre and the other tribal clans. Crops were not planted. Between the ravages of war and a prolonged drought, hunger spread.[21]

During the summer of 1992, Somalia took the short fall into outright lawlessness. Between two and three million people were starving. Heart-rending pictures and accounts made their way back to the United States and, as Americans are given to doing, we sent help. American and Coalition military forces began supporting civilian relief organizations as they distributed food. Because our guns were bigger than the warring clans' guns, we could provide security around and during the food distribution effort. That worked.

A new American presidential administration and the United Nations set out to use America's military presence to begin rebuilding a country in Somalia. That was a mistake if for no other reason than there probably never was a country in Somalia as we think of countries. Somalia was a mosaic of clans, poverty, and corruption. Military forces can provide a measure of order in a specific place for a period of time. In that place, for that time, communities and people and countries have the chance to regroup and rebuild. But they have to seize that chance for themselves and seize it with a purpose. No amount of military power can do that for them.

The American effort in Somalia came to grief. Images of a dead American soldier being dragged through the streets of Mogadishu by the people our forces were there to help caused a precipitous American withdrawal. Where we went off course in Somalia was in trying to use military power to set right a failed state. Military power can support a move toward freedom, but it cannot substitute for a people claiming their own freedom and their own future. We missed that painfully learned lesson going into the Iraq War and fell into the trap of trying to remake Iraq in an American image. The Iraqis can either build a country for themselves or not, but it is their task to do, not ours. The best military advice that President Bush received in the planning for the war was from his secretary of state, former General Colin Powell: if you break it, you own it.

Calling ourselves the world's sole superpower misleads more than it clarifies. Being a sole superpower means only that we are the best in the world at fighting the kind of battle we have chosen to fight, a high-tech conventional warfight. Our adversaries may choose to fight a different kind of war.

Even within the tactics of our choosing, we need to realistically understand where we are before we become enamored with our superpower self-description. In World War II, we had 40,000 heavy bombers. Today, we have 186 bombers and of those, almost all are either 1950s vintage B-52s or 1980s B-1 Cold War–era aircraft designed to penetrate Soviet air space and deliver nuclear weapons.[22] These older planes still have considerable utility, but only 20 of our bombers, the B-2s, are as modern to our era as the 40,000 were to theirs. The fighter numbers are the same. In World War II, we had 86,566 fighters.[23] Our current goal is to have 180 air-to-air F-22s and perhaps 1,000 air-to-ground F-35s replacing a larger number of F-16s.

There are obvious differences between our World War II needs and current requirements. World War II was a time of national peril that called forth a properly huge national effort. The 186 bombers and 1,200 fighters we have or plan to have are precision warfare capable and, airframe for airframe, dramatically more lethal. We certainly should not maintain a World War II level of forces now, but a fleet of 20 modern bombers is a rather modest fleet for a nation that casts itself as the world's sole superpower.

We have the dominant nuclear arsenal in the world and have cut it by more than half. Cutting is the correct approach, because a large and expensive nuclear triad now has little tactical value and a small, highly capable nuclear stockpile has as much strategic value as a large aging one. A workable missile defense system would be a valuable asset against the uncertain threat of the nuclear proliferation we know about, even more against the proliferation we don't know about.

We decreased the size of our military in response to the demise of the Soviet Union and the passing of the Cold War. That was also the right decision, but we should be mindful of emerging threats. China has approximately two and a half million soldiers on active duty (the United States has a half million), is modernizing its force, has a space program, and is a nuclear power. China appears to be building toward something like the navy that the United States formerly had: their fleet of warships will be larger than ours sometime around 2015 and will likely have three carrier battle groups.[24] China has spent heavily on quiet submarines, the specific capability that best competes with the U.S. Navy.[25] As China's economy grows, its military potential grows apace.

There are reasons—often sound reasons—for our limited military capabilities. But the phrase "sole superpower" conjures up an image of an America that can militarily dominate the world. That is a dangerous misconception that will fade quickly in the face of reality. It was never our purpose to militarily dominate the world: the purpose of our military is to defend America.

Our strength as a nation comes from our ideals and our values. America's success as a global power will come from those strengths, not from the lethality of our weapons systems. That is a good thing because those ideals and values are at the core of why there came to be an America and why America has succeeded. Remaining true to the fundamentals of America is a clear path ahead as a global power.

CHAPTER 11:
Dollar Power

AMERICA'S FIRST BATTLE OF WORLD WAR II had more to do with economics than with armaments. Japan's attack on Pearl Harbor in 1941 was less about numbers and capabilities of ships and airplanes than it was about Kansas wheat fields and Detroit auto factories.

Japan in the 1930s was a small nation with few natural resources that maintained itself at a stridently high level of military preparedness. America in the 1930s was a large nation with vast natural resources that maintained itself at a complacently low level of military preparedness. The Japanese fleet commander, Admiral Isoroku Yamamoto, had seen the industrial and agricultural potential of the United States when he was a naval attaché at the Japanese embassy in Washington and as a student at Harvard.[1] He saw the scope of America and the strength of its economy.[2] He understood the American capability, as yet untapped, for waging global war. Yamamoto thought that America, if given time, would overwhelm Japan in a war in the Pacific.

That was the genesis of the Pearl Harbor attack. Japan's plan was to deliver a knockout blow to the American fleet based there, consolidate their conquests in the Pacific and then hope for a negotiated settlement before America could mobilize and bring the war to Japan.[3] Hope, as American military officers are given to saying, is not a plan. Yamamoto was correct in his assessment of America's overwhelming military might when all of America goes to war. He came very close to success in destroying the American fleet at Pearl Harbor and gaining naval dominance in the Pacific, at least for the period of time he thought he needed. That did not matter. The Japanese ultra-nationalist leadership of the time was altogether wrong in their reading of the American character. An armistice was never an option.

Pearl Harbor brought all of America to war: its people, its economy, and its science. As a Japanese fleet admiral in 1941 was astute enough to realize, the power of America roused to war was overwhelming. America mobilized the best of its people and sent them to fight, retooled its economy to support the war, and redirected its science to win the war. Today, the Pentagon buys something between one hundred and two hundred airplanes a year. In 1944 alone, America produced more than ninety-six thousand airplanes for the war effort. The entire U.S. Navy is now fewer than three hundred ships, and each ship will be in the fleet for decades. The United States built more warships than that in both 1943 and 1944.[4] Today, the American flagged merchant marine consists of 242 ships. During the war, America built 5,800 such ships.[5]

Spending money on the right military technology is important. In the decade before World War II, France was widely thought to have the best army in the world. Based on their experiences in World War I, the French Army developed a strategy that included static defense. From 1930 to 1937, much of their effort and military budgets went into the fixed fortifications of the Maginot Line.[6] Their technology choice was poured concrete. They thought about and talked about heavy tank divisions but were still thinking and talking when the Germans invaded France in May 1940.[7]

The German Army came out of the same battles of World War I with a very different approach. They adopted a strategy of mechanized maneuver warfare. Their technology was tanks and truck-mounted infantry supported by close air support fighters and bombers. They could not afford to equip more than a small part of their army that way but what they did field, they fielded well.

These different approaches were tested when Germany invaded France. The poured concrete solution lost.

A similar technology transformation took place in both the British Royal Navy and the U.S. Navy. The rapidly expanding use of airplanes in World War I was not limited to ground-based aircraft. Both of the English-speaking navies saw the value of using airplanes as spotters for the battleships that were then the heart of their fleets. That meant planes somehow launched at sea: on pontoons or from catapults or off decks, or perhaps dirigibles or even aircraft launched from dirigibles. Ships of the day that might carry airplanes were called airplane carriers.[8] The Great War ended before these ideas jelled.

After World War I, American and British naval officers theorized about naval aviation, not just in the scout role it had but the attack role it might have. They skirted around treaty restrictions, built the ships and planes, trained the pilots, and wrote the doctrine for a new kind of naval aviation on the strength of what looked to be a good idea. When war came in the Pacific at Pearl Harbor, the U.S. Navy had aircraft carriers, the only kind of ship that could fight that war.[9]

In Europe, France lost the technology competition and slid into a trough of defeat and Vichy collaboration with Nazi Germany. In the Pacific, America kept pace with changing technologies and won.

America's Cold War success rested on the power of the American economy. Military power is expensive.

After World War II, Britain sought to regain its prewar position of influence and reclaimed the Mediterranean as a traditional sphere of British responsibility. That soon came to require economic and military support to the Greek government fighting a determined communist insurgency there. On an otherwise slow Friday afternoon at the State Department in Washington in 1947, Dean Acheson received a note from the British explaining that they were pulling out of the Med.[10] They were, in a word, broke. Britain was relinquishing its visions of glory and sending the Greek problem to the United States. Only America had the economic wherewithal to take up the task of opposing Soviet expansion, in Greece and elsewhere.

The Cold War turned out not to be a matter of whether America had a better military than the Soviet Union. Both sides fielded large and capable forces, both sides turned their science and technology to develop and maintain devastating nuclear capabilities. But in the end, there was no war: the Cold War was a contest of ideals and economic staying power.

Throughout the Cold War, the Soviet Union had a Third World economy struggling to support a superpower military establishment. America fielded a large force during the Cold War for about 6–9 percent of our gross domestic product (GDP). The Soviets were probably in the 20–30 percent GDP range, we were not sure which, then or now, and the Soviets probably did not know either.[11] Whatever their spending actually was, it was not sustainable. The implosion of the Soviet empire was first economic, then political, then military. No amount of military power can generate a robust, self-sustaining economy.

Renewing America's military might requires rethinking our defense funding. We now have a budget on auto pilot unconnected to any coherent strategy. Until we build a strategy and link that strategy to our funding, we won't know whether we are spending too much money, spending too little money, or spending money in the wrong places.

Events have a way of clarifying spending levels. In World War II, when the freedom and sovereignty of the United States hung in the balance, we spent an incredible 37 percent of our GDP on defense.[12] Given the track record and ambitions of Nazi Germany and Imperial Japan, that was money well spent.

During the Cold War, when the Soviet Union was aiming thousands of nuclear warheads at America and had an army poised to invade Western Europe, we fielded a large and capable military. When John Kennedy was president, 50 percent of the federal budget went to defense: that proved to have been about the right level of top line spending for the threat we faced at the time. We are now spending 4 percent of our GDP and just 20 percent of the federal budget on defense.[13]

Within that available defense spending, we have made some otherwise sound decisions that have put our Pentagon budget in disarray. For much of the Cold War, our military forces were manned with draftees who received a pittance of a wage. Service was regarded as service; there was no thought that it required competitive compensation. Today, our all-volunteer force must have wages comparable to the civilian sector, or they won't volunteer. As we are currently structured, expanding the army significantly when a major war comes will be difficult or impossible.

Our force now is also a married force. Quality of life issues, such as housing, on-post day care and recreational facilities, must be funded. As a result of these trends, the total personnel cost of our much smaller force takes a much larger slice of the Pentagon budget: something on the order of four-fifths of our army budget goes to our people costs.[14] And we are not just paying for what we get, we are paying for what we got: a quarter of our pay and allowance budget goes to retirement benefits paid after the soldier, sailor, airman, or marine leaves the service.[15]

Another sound decision that has wreaked havoc on the Pentagon budget is precision warfare. Precision is the right operational approach, but it is expensive. We are spending two billion dollars apiece on bombers, three billion a copy for the proposed new destroyer, and ten billion for the next aircraft carrier.[16] We buy fewer and fewer of these big ticket items, but the capital outlay is still burdensome.

Our lack of a strategy-to-spending connection has driven the Pentagon to poor stewardship of much of the funding it does get. We have borrowed from long-term equipment modernization and research and development accounts to pay short-term bills for things like fuel, salary, and ammunition. Even with no big expenditures like the air force's F-22, the army is 20 percent short of being able to pay its bills every year. When the money does not come in, here is what happens:

• The army builds new barracks and then can't fund their routine maintenance. Those buildings then age at twice the rate they should. Some of our troops are living under leaky roofs.

• Our equipment gets older, breaks down more often, and costs more to operate. Those costs are increasing 10 percent a year and have for the last several years. That situation is going to get worse.

• We are a capital-based military, dependent on modern equipment and new technology, but we are not re-capitalizing our force. Not only are we not buying the new equipment we need, given the wear and tear on our forces in Iraq, we cannot even afford to maintain the equipment we have.

To make matters still worse, there are new bills coming due: a national missile defense system and the increasing health care costs associated with expanded veterans' benefits. Both of these new expenditures are many billions of dollars a year now, both will grow, and both must come from an already overdrawn checking account. When an event like the long-term counterinsurgency in Iraq comes along, research, new equipment, training, and maintenance accounts are further depleted to pay the costs of the effort.

Our budget breakdown came about when we went from a known, predictable strategy in the Cold War of defending Europe from a Soviet invasion into a time of change, confusion, and learn-as-you-go missions. The certainty of defending Western Europe was replaced by the uncertainty of peacekeeping, peace making, peace enforcement, humanitarian missions, engagement, homeland defense, counter-terrorism, and regional conventional wars. In a forty-year Cold War, a six- to eight-year procurement cycle to refurbish tanks was acceptable. It doesn't work now: for precision warfare information technology that has a shelf life of several years at most, a six-year procurement cycle means that the more money we spend, the further behind we get.

If anyone doubts that the Pentagon budgets by bureaucracy rather than by strategy, be aware that the army share of the overall defense budget today is 24 percent. Thirty-five years ago, it was 24 percent. Every year for the last thirty-five years, it has hovered around 24 percent.[17] In that time, we have fought wars, abolished the draft, ended the Cold War, technology has gone vertical, and the military missions we face have changed dramatically. If budget decisions had any relation to reality and the exercise of sound judgment, surely that 24 percent would have gone up or down or done something other than remain static. In this Pentagon turf truce, which even the most aggressive secretaries of defense have been loath to challenge, the other services' budgets have been similarly locked in place. And these estimates are just estimates: Pentagon bookkeeping would make an Enron accountant blush. The Pentagon is often unsure of what gets spent where and is usually unsure of the results of that spending.

The post–Cold War force we have and the equipment it gets are not strategic decisions. We are where we are because that is where the budget has taken us. The size of our force, our equipment, and our equipment-fielding schedules are decisions made by government budgeteers and politicians, not generals. Instead of budgeting for the force we need, we have the force that fits our budget. At times, we operate the process exactly in reverse: Congress will earmark funding to buy equipment that the Pentagon does not think it needs if the equipment means jobs in a powerful member's home district. The Pentagon then must man and maintain the equipment and attempt to devise a strategy that uses it. Sometimes they don't even try. After a decent interval, the equipment is given or sold at a deep discount to Third World countries.

In the post–Cold War lull, the United States has not gone to war unless we chose to go to war. We now have the option of spending less money and effort on our current warfight and more on our future warfight. That is not just more and better technology: it includes developing the next strategy, re-tethering our military to our citizens, and rebalancing our forces between a standing military and citizen soldiers. These are policy decisions that will drive the budget rather than continuing to allow the budget to paint us into policy corners.

The Washington conventional wisdom is that the United States is the world's sole superpower and that no peer competitor will emerge to threaten that dominance for at least a decade. We need to be cautious here. During the 1920s and early 1930s, Great Britain was the reigning world power. A series of British governments looking for reasons to cut defense spending came up with something called the ten-year rule. The idea was that if the government would certify that no major war like World War I would occur for ten years, Britain would defer fully funding defense for another year—and then restart the ten-year rule. A parade of British ministers came before Parliament and avowed that all was safe for the coming decade.[18]

When Hitler re-armed Germany, built a navy and an offensive air force and army, Britain's ten-year rule proved to have been a legislated head start for the German war effort. Despite Winston Churchill's intemperate warnings, as war approached, England was woefully unprepared. The Soviet Union could field three hundred army divisions, Germany two hundred, France and Italy a hundred each. Even Czechoslovakia, sacrificed by Britain and France at Munich in 1938, had forty trained and equipped divisions when it was delivered over to Hitler. Six months before Britain went to war with Germany in 1939, it could field a total of eight divisions on the continent.[19]

America cannot afford a ten-year rule hiatus. The British in the 1930s at least required a decision to certify that no major war was in the offing. The United States now requires only that a blind eye be turned to the problem.

There is significant risk involved in reworking our defense spending. The Pentagon will get some of it wrong, but business as usual will not fix this problem. What will fix this problem is to align our strategy and our resources. That means deciding what the threats to our national interests really are, devising a strategy to meet those threats, and then building the forces to execute that strategy. It may mean more or less money than we are currently spending, it may mean spending money on different things. Until we think through what we are trying to do and how to do it, we won't know.

CHAPTER 12:
Generals and Admirals

Renewing America's military might includes dusting off some musty items from America's attic. The very term "officer corps" has a faint odor of history about it and seems somehow out of step with electrons and precision warfare and spaced-based systems. It isn't. Our officer corps, particularly our generals and admirals, are the source of one of the wellsprings of our past success—strategic vision—and are the stewards of another, the values shared between our citizens and our soldiers. Our senior officer values are passed on, knowingly and on purpose, from one generation of officers to the next.

Dwight Eisenhower, a general who knew a great deal about weapons and war, commanded the military forces of all Allied nations in Europe in World War II. After the defeat of Germany, Eisenhower wrote with feeling that the strongest weapon he had throughout the war years was the unflinching support of Army Chief of Staff George Marshall.[1] Eisenhower meant it and meant it literally. That is not the sort of thing field commanders normally say about staff people, and it is worth knowing why Eisenhower did.

In 1939, the American army and its air corps numbered fewer than two hundred thousand soldiers and airmen, had little equipment, and the equipment it did have was obsolete. Despite the fact that Europe had been in a state of military crisis for the better part of the decade, despite the fact that Japan had been invading countries in Asia since the early 1930s, the U.S. Army was woefully unprepared for war.[2]

George Marshall changed that. He was sworn in as chief of staff on September 1, 1939, by coincidence, the very day Hitler invaded Poland and started the war in earnest. The Japanese attack on Pearl Harbor in December 1941 brought the war suddenly to America's door. The most grievous threat that America faced was Germany bestride a conquered Europe. Marshall developed a strategy to meet that threat: conduct a cross-channel invasion to defeat the Germans in land warfare in Europe while waging a defensive campaign in the Pacific against Japan.[3] Then he built the force to fight that fight: army divisions and army air forces with both tactical power and strategic reach.

Almost everyone else had a different strategy. American and English air generals wanted to bomb Germany into submission. They tried. It did not work and would not have worked. German war production remained robust, despite two years of sustained bombing, as the Allied armies reached the German border. America's admirals wanted to fight Germany by defeating Japan in a naval campaign in the Pacific. That did not work and would not have worked. Something on the order of 15 percent of America's war effort was made in the Pacific, so an early defeat of Japan would have had limited impact on the war in Europe.[4]

Although the British shared the goal of defeating Germany, they had yet another strategy in mind. Britain's war leader, Winston Churchill, wanted to restore his country's prewar eminence. Churchill's war, if he got to choose, would be operations in the Mediterranean, in Sicily, in the Balkans, attacks against weak spots at the periphery of the German conquests.[5] Britain had in truth lost a generation in the mud of Flanders fields in World War I. In four years of war, Great Britain lost a million soldiers. The United States lost 50,280 and was in serious combat for only four months.[6] Britain did not have the manpower to bear the losses of sustained ground combat in another world war inside twenty-five years.

Marshall's strategy prevailed, and he then set about raising the army America needed. He and Roosevelt first convinced Congress that the nation needed a draft. They were successful, but just. The extension of the one-year draft law in August 1941, four months before Pearl Harbor, passed Congress by a single vote.[7] Marshall's well-known adherence to old army values of integrity and candor was crucial. When Roosevelt struggled with Congress on critical issues like the need for a draft, sending scarce military equipment to Britain to keep her in the war, or seeking massive funding to develop an atomic bomb without disclosing to Congress what the funding was for, he dispatched Marshall to Capitol Hill.[8] The members of Congress would believe Marshall when they would not credit the word of an admittedly wily president.

As war approached, Marshall called eighteen National Guard divisions to active duty.[9] After Pearl Harbor, there was a rush of citizens to arms: December 8, 1941, remains the largest recruiting day in America's history.[10] When these citizen soldiers, these Guardsmen and draftees and volunteers began reporting in, Marshall knew what to do with them. He knew both the war that lay ahead and the army that America must have to fight it.

Marshall was a Pershing protégé and had served in key positions in Europe in World War I. He had helped mobilize young men for the Civilian Conservation Corps in the 1930s and had learned more about citizen soldiers when a vengeful Douglas MacArthur banished him to the Illinois National Guard when MacArthur became chief of staff.[11] Marshall knew he couldn't take American civilians and force them into a regular army mold. Citizen soldiers are not regular soldiers of lesser skill: they are citizens in uniform, fighting for their country in times of crisis. They bring initiative, values, and the heart of America with them when they go to war. One of Marshall's towering strengths was his ability to take regular army standards for soldiering and old army values and build a citizen soldier army. That is what won him Churchill's accolade as the organizer of victory.[12]

Marshall also knew something that Ulysses S. Grant knew: Americans go to war to defend their country. Grant described them as "the men who risk life for a principle."[13] Marshall built an army on that knowledge. German officers took an oath not to Germany, not to Hitler as head of state, but to Hitler personally. American soldiers take an oath to defend the Constitution. That Constitution is itself just another piece of paper, it is the ideas in it that American soldiers defend.

The American force that helped liberate Europe was Marshall's army fighting a strategy Marshall devised under leaders that Marshall selected. That is why its field commander, Dwight Eisenhower, wrote that Marshall's support was his most potent weapon. Marshall brought the strategic insight and leadership that allowed America to find victory. The skills and values that Marshall had in such great measure were passed on to the senior officers that followed him, Eisenhower and Bradley and Ridgway, among others. They reside today in our flag officers as well.

The role of our officer corps now has become less clear because our military's purpose has become less clear.[14] Americans have traditionally viewed their armed forces as warfighters, the defenders of America's freedom. Now those forces must also be a paramilitary arm of the Red Cross or a heavily armed police force for the United Nations. Those are worthwhile missions and meet the needs of the times, but the lengthening list of tasks other than warfighting has clouded the reason why there is an American profession of arms in the first place, the calling to fight and win wars.

There are other trends challenging our officers. Large parts of how we now run the military have been co-opted from the business world. That makes sense in many cases, but in the final analysis, war is not a business. The media and the Internet, as they have with all professions, have taken some of the mystique from the profession of arms. Disseminating information about military events and issues is almost always a good idea. American military operations now routinely have reporters and camera people maneuvering with our units in the field: instant video of combat as it happens fills the airwaves with information, but information is not necessarily knowledge. And we now make decisions and act through an often dysfunctional bureaucracy. If we send a few hundred soldiers overseas on an engagement mission, more than a few hundred headquarters staffers and civilians will review, approve, and monitor that force. That makes decisive and timely action very difficult.

An issue of some concern is how our officer corps should respond in this era of ambiguous missions, media scrutiny, and bureaucratic decision making. Are officers to be warriors who run the risk of being isolated or better bureaucrats more adept within the Washington way of making decisions? This is not wool gathering in the abstract. Many Western European countries have already shifted their officer corps to a sort of uniformed civil service.

That is dramatically the wrong approach. Our officers must safeguard the values that allow us to win wars and keep our military forces firmly within the American experience. Our officers become bureaucrats at their peril and our loss.

★ ★ ★ ★

Becoming a general is like catching lightning in a bottle. There is nothing quite like it in civilian life. Of the two thousand army full colonels that are considered for brigadier general each year, only the top thirty-five make it—but the second thirty-five were just as good. And the third and probably the fourth thirty-five as well. One of the bits of wisdom I was told after making flag rank is that every screw-up that a general walks past without correcting becomes the new standard. Having that level of responsibility for one of the very best parts of America is a gift.

The way we pick our flag officers is important. We do that now with rites of passage. Once a year behind closed doors in the bowels of the Pentagon, the four military services each hold selection boards to pick their top colonels and navy captains to become brigadier generals or rear admirals. The army selection board reviews records that show a remarkably similar catechism of career paths. Basic branch qualification school as a new lieutenant, platoon leader, company command, branch advanced schooling for a year, staff assignments, command and general staff college for another year, battalion command for two years, the war college for a year, Pentagon staff duty, brigade command for two years. That is a quarter-century of doing the same thing as the other colonels being considered for flag rank.

One thing we can do better is to assure that, every now and then, some non-routine officers with non-routine experiences slip through those wickets and become generals. Some of our very best leaders had experiences out of the mainstream as young officers. George Patton competed in the 1912 Olympics.[15] Dwight Eisenhower journeyed with the first truck convoy to go from one coast of America to the other in 1919.[16] Jimmy Doolittle was flying in air races between the world wars when that was both ridiculously dangerous and a national preoccupation.[17] That kind of cowboy flying helped him lead the supremely unorthodox mission of flying army bombers off a navy carrier for the Doolittle raid against Tokyo in 1942, the first blow of an America coming back from defeat at Pearl Harbor. Officers' career paths were much less structured then and much less full. An officer today can barely get all the mandatory requirements into the quarter-century before he or she is considered for flag rank. And most of the things our officers formerly were able to do would now be seen as diversions or setbacks.

We need to lighten up and loosen up, to let our young officers go do some out of the ordinary things. We cannot predict the skills we will need in the future with anything like the precision we impose on our current career gates. Would a year at Microsoft help? A year in the oil fields of the Caspian region before we go to war there? A year working with developing nations and the non-governmental organizations that populate our engagement activities? A year assigned to our reserve components, which, as it was in Marshall's era, is still considered a career death sentence?

Yes, in fact. They all would.

An out of left field career that worked was that of Gen. John J. Pershing, who was the commander of the American Expeditionary Forces in France in World War I. Pershing is a general who has slipped into a fold in our history and is less well known than he should be. Pershing was the first captain of cadets at West Point, got a law degree while on ROTC assignment at Nebraska, and was an observer of the Russo-Japanese War in 1904. Pershing was promoted from captain directly to brigadier general. Frustrated by the iron grip of seniority on army promotions and lobbied by Pershing's father-in-law (a prominent senator), Theodore Roosevelt skipped Pershing over three ranks and much of the American officer corps. It was a good choice. In 1916, the best that the U.S. Army could do in the punitive expedition into Mexico against Villa, an operation commanded by Pershing, was to field a force of ten thousand troops and rely on horse cavalry as the dominant arm. By 1918, Pershing understood the organization and logistics required for massive armies of millions of soldiers and he built, trained, and fielded that kind of force in France. We should not let our career milestones become as rigid as the seniority system that plagued Pershing.

Generals and admirals in the Pentagon have to be a mix of warrior and courtier. Warrior because only senior flag officers have the professional background to advise presidents and secretaries of defense on going to war and fighting wars. Courtiers because they have to make their way in the bureaucratic back alleys of civilian policymaking in the Pentagon, at the White House, and on Capitol Hill. It is a difficult balance to get right. Any number of good warfighting flag officers have been reluctant to accept assignments to the Pentagon, where they would have to hone courtier skills. That is unfortunate, because it is important to have credible warfighters in place: without their counsel, civilians who have responsibility for defense decisions will be poorly advised. The challenge to senior officers is to be enough of a courtier to be asked for counsel and listened to and enough of a warrior to give well founded and forthright advice.

Every senior flag officer has more than three decades of successful military experience to qualify them to have an opinion. Only the best qualified get to the top and that at enormous effort and with lottery-winning levels of good fortune. Once there, our generals and admirals carry the lessons of America's wars every day and for every decision. They wear ribbons on their chest so that no one forgets the source of their authority when they speak.

Civilian officials in the Pentagon carry a different brief. They are just as smart as senior uniformed officers, love their country just as much, and try just as hard. But they know little of war. They are in office to develop and defend the policies of a particular presidential administration. When presidents worry about politics, secretaries of defense worry about politics. Generals and admirals don't and that is where it gets complicated.

The split between civilians and generals became painfully clear during Matthew Ridgway's storm-tossed two-year term as army chief of staff in the mid-1950s. Ridgway represented an infantry-heavy army in an era when the prevailing wisdom was that future wars would be fought by the air force and won with nuclear weapons. Year in and year out, Pentagon budgets reflected that pronounced air power bias and nuclear reliance. Ridgway refused to publicly endorse that approach and, as a result of his independence, was allowed to retire early.[18]

In his final report as chief of staff, given as he left the army, Ridgway offered the view that senior uniformed officers must be allowed, indeed encouraged, to give their unvarnished advice on military matters, ignoring the political winds of any given presidential administration. That was and is a serious issue. The Eisenhower New Look defense approach of air power dominance was not just politics, it was a knowledgeable president's hard and fast policy. Ridgway thought it was wrong and, within the Pentagon and at the White House, said so. Eisenhower and Secretary of Defense Charles Wilson wanted senior officers who would publicly tout the administration's views regardless of their own opinion.

This is more than just a history lesson, something else from America's attic: forthright senior officer counsel is critical to success, and the absence of that counsel is crippling. The war in Vietnam cried out for senior officer policy dissent but little was forthcoming. For Vietnam, no general was disruptive enough to be fired and no general resigned. If ever that should have happened, it should have happened during the long war in Vietnam. There were hints and rumors and feints of resignation but it never occurred. There is a lingering story in our officer corps that an army chief of staff actually got in his car and was driven to the White House to resign. When he got there, he changed his mind and was driven back to the Pentagon. That officer was General Harold K. Johnson. Johnson was a POW in World War II and survived the Bataan Death March. POW's rank with Medal of Honor winners for status within the military. On top of that, General Johnson was widely known for his integrity. In his latter years, he viewed his decision not to resign over Vietnam with anguish.[19]

For the run-up to the Iraq War, policy dissent by senior officers was aggressively and publicly squelched by Pentagon and White House civilians. Events proved the dissent to have been right, the secretary of defense and the president to have been wrong. During the war, the combatant commander with responsibility for the war in Iraq was either fired or resigned—it is unclear which, and it makes little difference—over strategy issues.[20] Whatever happened, his resignation reflects an inability of our current way of doing business to deal well with divergent views from senior officers.

Every senior officer in the Pentagon faces Ridgway-type decisions. This is one of those areas where civilian control of the military includes defining the terms by which military advice is sought and used by presidents. Lack of trust between senior officers and senior civilians cuts the flow of good advice to a trickle. That happened with Vietnam and it happened with Iraq. Few generals and admirals fully understand the civilian concerns that weigh on presidents and their secretaries of defense. Few civilian officials fully understand wars and how they are fought. A candid give and take on these issues is most likely to yield the right answer, and that kind of discourse occurs only at the sufferance of civilians.

Generals get to be generals by leading from the front. How that works in the army can be seen in airborne operations. The troops roll out early, well before the sun comes up. They load themselves and their combat gear on trucks and move to the still dark airfield. There they are briefed on what is going to happen on the aircraft en route, the size and shape of the drop zone, and where and how to assemble after they land. They put on parachutes, and each gets a hands-on check by a jumpmaster. About every third word is a deep bark that sounds like HUOAH. No one knows exactly what that word means or where it came from, but it gets used a lot. The marines have a similar grunt that sounds like a dog barking.

The big air force transport aircraft takes off and flies for an hour or two, and then the air force flight crew opens the rear doors of the airplane. The wind and noise are enveloping, the energy level spikes. The jumpmaster goes through a series of commands to get the troops lined up, hooked up to a cable that runs the length of the aircraft over their heads, and ready to go. It is an operational ritual and, because it becomes familiar, becomes comforting in the wind and noise and lurching aircraft.

But there is always an air of controlled tension during a jump. Despite the ritual and bravado, the HUOAHs and the swagger, the fact remains that a lot of soldiers are getting ready to jump from an aircraft in flight. As they get close to the drop zone, the jumpmaster puts his first jumper in the door. The signal light by the open door of the airplane goes from red to green and each soldier moves quickly to the door and throws himself out of the airplane. In an instant, they are gone.

In the American army, the first jumper out the door is often a senior officer who has little or no operational requirement to be there. To keep generals from killing themselves indiscriminately, the vice chief of staff, the number two man in the army, grants specific by name/ by jump approval for all jump-qualified generals not assigned to an airborne unit. We have generals who blithely ignore this regulation. The air force has similar provisions about generals flying airplanes. It is a good thing to have senior officers that must be reined in on high-risk operations. Those are the officers who set the example for our forces.

The lineage of our flag officers is laced with that kind of spirit. George Washington showed it under fire, rallying his retreating troops back into battle at Monmouth.[21] Grant in the Civil War declined his staff's urgent request to leave the hill from which he was observing a battle because the Confederate infantry was preparing to attack. Grant instead told his staff to bring up artillery and hold the hill.[22] MacArthur showed that same spirit in World War I, standing above a trench line under enemy fire talking casually with George Patton.[23] Eisenhower as a four-star general folded himself into a makeshift seat in the back of a P-51 and flew with the commanding general of his tactical air command over German lines.[24] James Gavin fought as an infantryman on the night drop into Normandy in World War II.[25] Creighton Abrams showed that spirit at Bastogne, in Vietnam, and in the Pentagon. A recent chairman of the JCS routinely went on military free fall jumps: that means an exit at twenty thousand feet, an oxygen mask, and a series of tasks to perform to make a happy ending more likely.

We want our generals saying HUOAH, even in the Pentagon. Perhaps especially in the Pentagon. There are ground rules: generals and admirals never have the option of opposing a president. They always have the obligation to be the bearer of bad tidings to the president.

Senior officer input to presidents is crucial and we have failed at this in the past. Douglas MacArthur, as America's Far East commander during the Korean War, pursued a strategy that was in conflict with President Truman's view of how to fight the war. MacArthur's strategy was to reignite the revolution in China, to invade the Chinese mainland with Chiang Kai-shek's Nationalist Chinese forces, which had fled to the island of Taiwan. MacArthur wanted to disrupt the Chinese military support that was sustaining the otherwise defeated North Koreans and was prepared to use America's nuclear arsenal to do that. He also proposed to "sow nuclear materials" across the border between North Korea and China to stop the flow of Chinese forces into battle.[26] As a matter of science, that made no sense, but it did indicate how far MacArthur was willing to widen the war.

MacArthur was seriously out of step with his president. MacArthur had been chief of staff of the army in the 1930s, the only four-star general in the army, when Eisenhower and Patton and Ridgway were captains and majors. He disobeyed clear orders from President Hoover in routing the Bonus Army of World War I veterans from their Washington encampment in 1932. MacArthur left the U.S. Army to become a field marshal in the Philippine Army, a comic opera position, and he was recalled to active duty in the U.S. Army in World War II.[27] After the war, he served as the American proconsul in postwar Japan and had an emperor at his beck and call. All of which gave MacArthur a uniquely lofty view of the world and his place it.

Instead of seeing Truman as his commander-in-chief, MacArthur seems to have seen just a former haberdasher, a very Main Street American from Missouri, put in the Senate by a corrupt political machine and an accidental president who came to the White House upon the death of the aristocratic Franklin Roosevelt. What MacArthur should have seen was the artillery captain who took part in the Muese Argonne offensive in World War I. He should have seen the president who ordered the use of atomic weapons that ended World War II, the president who had stared down labor unions, confronted Stalin with the Berlin airlift, and won a presidential election few thought he could win.

MacArthur sought to widen the war in Korea to the point that America would mobilize and win it. This was MacArthur's third war as a general: his first two were world wars in which America's effort was limited largely by the size of our manpower pool and our industrial capacity. The war in Korea was limited by presidential judgment. In pursuing a strategy different than the president's, MacArthur undertook diplomatic initiatives, complete with press releases, that clearly fell within a president's prerogatives. Matters came to a head when MacArthur was caught undermining Truman's position in a letter to an influential congressman. Eisenhower, who had been MacArthur's aide for six years, later wrote that the stringent army practice of avoiding politics was not part of MacArthur's make-up.[28]

Some statements sound so grand that they ought to be true. MacArthur's magnificent phrase, "There is no substitute for victory," falls in that category. Capturing the frustration of the American experience in Korea, MacArthur's words strike a deep cord. But he was wrong. Absent a massive use of America's nuclear weapons and the attendant massive loss of life, the war in Korea was not winnable. A stalemate in a limited war was preferable to an all-out war with the Soviet Union or China where victory was unattainable on anything approaching acceptable terms. Truman, and later President Eisenhower, understood that. MacArthur did not.[29]

★ ★ ★ ★

Senior officer counsel to presidents has worked in our past. In 1954, the French were trying to restore their colonial dominion in Indochina and things were going very badly after seven years of war. The Vietnamese opposition to French colonial rule—the Viet Minh—were communist and during the Cold War that fact alone was sufficient to determine which side America supported. Two members of the Joints Chiefs of Staff—Twining of the air force and JCS Chairman Radford of the navy—were pressing for an air-power-alone-can-win American intervention to rescue the failing French effort.[30]

The French had an army in Vietnam designed for conventional war in Europe. Their forces were dependent on roads, which were few in Vietnam, and on air resupply that was tenuous at best. The Vietnamese communists evolved their insurgent guerilla force into a conventional army suited to the terrain and the war they were fighting: the Viet Minh used porters for much of their transport and locally gathered supplies where they could. The Viet Minh conventional war capabilities went unnoticed or were discounted by the French.

Matters reached a crisis level when a French force parachuted into a remote area of northern Vietnam, repaired a derelict airstrip, and built a series of defensive strong points at Dien Bien Phu. Their strategy was to entice the Vietnamese insurgents to attack them. The French got their wish but had seriously underestimated their enemy: the garrison at Dien Bien Phu was soon cut off and surrounded. Air resupply was reduced and then all but eliminated. French legionnaires, shades of Beau Geste, were facing a teeming native army. If the French were to be saved from the strategic blunder of their generals, it was America that would have to save them.[31] General Twining and Admiral Radford were proposing American air strikes around Dien Bien Phu, including the use of nuclear weapons, to stave off a French defeat.[32]

Matthew Ridgway, following his success in Korea, became army chief of staff in 1953. Having just fought a land war in Asia, he was much less enthused than the air generals about the wisdom of an American intervention in Vietnam. Without so much as a by your leave from anyone, he dispatched a team of army officers to assess the scope of an American war there. What the Ridgway team found was not encouraging. A war in Vietnam would be an infantry war, won or lost on the ground. That kind of war would take a half million American troops and last ten years and would in all likelihood be a very difficult war. The U.S. Army was, if anything, more conventional than the French. There were not adequate ports, roads, airfields, nor infrastructure to support an American military deployment. The United States would have to build them. The Ridgway assessment was dramatically different from the air strike proposals being offered by Twining and Radford. It mattered to Ridgway that the force at Dien Bien Phu was a mercenary army of French Foreign Legionnaires: France declined to send the draftees of its own army to Indochina.[33] Ridgway could see no reason to substitute American conscripts.

Ridgway had been one of President Eisenhower's senior ground commanders in Europe during World War II and the two had been friends for more than three decades.[34] Ridgway met with Eisenhower and laid out his Vietnam findings. Eisenhower probably knew more about theater logistics than all of the Joint Chiefs combined, certainly more than Twining and Radford. Despite his fondness for air power and the relatively modest defense budgets it allowed, Eisenhower saw the sense of the Ridgway position.[35] There was no American rescue of the French.

Ridgway's opposition to a war in Vietnam was part and parcel of his ongoing questioning of Eisenhower's New Look defense policies that gave the air force and navy primacy over the army. This was not a MacArthur-type effort to subvert a presidential decision. Ridgway was pressing his strongly held professional views as defense policies were being developed. He was an unrelenting advocate for what he viewed as a sensible role for the army.

When Ridgway's contentious and abbreviated term as army chief of staff ended in 1955, his replacement was Maxwell Taylor. Taylor would become one of the principal architects of America's policy in

Vietnam. As a part of his selection process for the chief's job, Taylor was summoned to Washington and given something of a loyalty interview by Secretary of Defense Wilson and President Eisenhower. After MacArthur's dismissal from command and Ridgway's recalcitrance over policy matters, the Eisenhower administration wanted someone that would support their positions. Not an unreasonable approach, but loyalty oaths had not been a matter of course in the military.[36] Whatever Taylor told them, it was sufficiently comforting for him to get the job.[37]

★ ★ ★ ★

A question that civilians ought to be asking about our uniformed leaders is do we have generals and admirals today that can be as good as Grant and Pershing, Marshall and Nimitz and Arnold. The answer is that we do—as good and perhaps better. The missions and operations our generals face today are more complex than ever before. War and engagement missions are now broadcast live as they happen to a watching world. Expectations are for quick victory with no or few casualties. The performance bar for today's flag officers has been raised.

Our future generals must understand the strengths of our past leaders. Where George Marshall and his World War II generation were particularly strong was in knowing and living our values. It was those core values that let Marshall hold his own with Franklin Roosevelt, let Eisenhower keep Patton in command in the midst of a press furor after Patton's atrocious behavior in slapping a soldier, and allowed Matthew Ridgway to win battles in Korea and help avoid a war in Vietnam in 1954.

There is a randomness to greatness among generals. Had there not been a World War II, Eisenhower, instead of being president, would have retired as an obscure army colonel.[38] There will be times and places where American generals and admirals will have to meet the moment. If we ensure that our flag officers bring the same commitment to values as their predecessors, coupled with their own high level of professional skill, we will not be found wanting for generalship.

The worst thing that can happen to our current and future generals and admirals is to become politicized. Unfortunately, that has become an issue despite a long and strong tradition to the contrary. For officers serving in the Pentagon, the presidency is institutionalized. Generals and admirals don't usually use a president's name, more from convention than from reverence. It is "the White House" or "across the river" or "POTUS" (President Of The United States). Even the first lady is given a rather unappealing acronym: FLOTUS. Politics is not an issue for uniformed officers at the highest levels, even behind the most closed of doors.

The distance between serving flag officers and partisan politics was narrowed when former four-stars began endorsing presidential candidates. Some retired officers are convinced that they did not relinquish their rights as citizens when they donned a uniform, even less so when they take off that uniform. They have a point. Debate on defense issues is better informed by their thoughts, but there is a price to be paid.

Civilians in each new administration are not knowledgeable about military mores. During presidential campaigns, they see recently retired generals and admirals supporting their opponent, so they go get some of their own. Retired senior officers have become campaign chits. It was inescapable that some tar would hit the still serving officers, one general looks much like another to civilians. Because political campaign supporters show up as cabinet and sub-cabinet appointees and as White House staffers, the distinction between still serving generals and recently retired generals gets lost in the rush of events.

The slippery slope of politics for senior officers has gotten a lot more slippery. The practice now is for our senior flag officers still on active duty to publicly endorse civilian defense decisions without reservation. The danger is that those decisions have become increasingly partisan. As a result, senior officer input now routinely becomes politicized.

How generals fighting wars get their orders has also changed and the trend is not helpful. During the critical first days of the Battle of the Bulge, Army Chief of Staff George Marshall did not contact Eisenhower, and he ordered the Pentagon not to contact Eisenhower's staff.[39] The Battle of the Bulge was among the largest battles the U.S. Army ever fought. The ubiquitous newspaper maps showing Allied battle lines advancing left to right across Europe were suddenly moving right to left. But Marshall, despite a close mentor/protégé relationship with Eisenhower, was wise enough to understand that Eisenhower, on the scene and in command, was more likely to make the correct decisions needed than would anyone in Washington. No one in the White House would have thought of contacting their European Theater commander directly. Left to their own devices, Eisenhower and Bradley and Patton not only won the battle but also inflicted a near fatal defeat on the German Army.

By Vietnam, the Pentagon and the White House were in the mode of helping. Messages, inquiries, and suggestion were always numerous and reached flood stage on occasion. Visits from Alexander Haig, Richard Nixon's favorite general, were frequent.

For Desert Storm, the system was brought to some semblance of sanity because the president, a World War II combat veteran, stayed his hand and his staff. The JCS chairman acted as a gatekeeper for White House inquiries and input. Even there, it was touch and go on occasion. A first-rate documentary about the Civil War by Ken Burns was airing on television during the Persian Gulf build-up. Lincoln's problems with General George McClellan's lack of aggressiveness became a newly minted bit of wisdom on the White House staff. One of these staffers reviewing the Desert Storm campaign plan compared Schwarzkopf to McClellan. Schwarzkopf, who had a habit of direct expression, heard about the less-than-flattering comparison. Colin Powell's traffic cop/soother-of-rough-edges role was taxed, but in the end it all worked.[40]

For the Iraq War, the trend to command by civilian committee took firm hold. Senior joint staff officers had to go hat in hand to the secretary of defense to get even the smallest unit on deployment orders. The secretary of defense held video teleconferences with the ground commander in Iraq. White House staffers made grand phubah visits to the combat zone. Even moderate-sized deployments now must have a full-time, fully staffed VIP visitors section to handle the traffic. Such visits are a daily event, and each and every visitor steals time and attention from the commander and his principal staff officers.

Generals and admirals still on active service can do little to correct the trend toward civilianized and politicized defense decision making. Civilians set the ground rules for senior officer input. The solution is civilian officials who put the good of the nation ahead of their own reelection prospects and let everyone know of their priorities. The solution is also senior officers who have the knowledge to frame hard choices and an enthusiasm for pressing those choices home.

If all else fails, generals can resign.

That occasionally happens. Within the last few years, a service chief of staff took a position in support of one of his field commanders who had been found wanting by a blue ribbon commission. The issue was one on which reasonable people could differ: the commission was well-led and made a strong case. The service chief thought they were wrong. The secretary of defense sided with the commission and the chief of staff sided with his field commander. The general resigned.[41] The story may not have made it much past the flag officers that pay attention to such things, but it was well received. He probably didn't say HOUAH, definitely didn't bark, but his actions spoke volumes.

A recent chief of staff of the army also got it right, fortunately well short of resignation. In the midst of renegotiating roles and missions with an energetic set of civilian leaders, the chief gave his senior generals some clear direction: everything is on the table except our values. It did not matter that all the army's missions were up for discussion. It did matter that none of our values were.

A fact about our flag officers that escapes civilian scrutiny is that we have too many generals and that the ones we have wear too many stars. The comparison that is normally offered to gauge this issue is that for our World War II army and army air force of more than 8 million people, we had 1,500 or so general officers. For our current active-duty army and air force of 800,000, we have 575 active-duty generals. A tenth of the force and a third as many generals.

That look back is catching at first glance but we don't have a World War II army and air force or a World War II mission. The answer to how many generals we need now is in the details. Something approaching 90 percent of our current flag officers are in staff or headquarters positions, put at flag rank to match some other services' or some other NATO nation's staff grade inflation. This is a sort of competitive self-levitation that has little relevance to our current force structure or mission set. When the Pentagon decided to revamp its procurement agency for Iraq, it designated three flag officer billets for the effort. We should reverse these trends toward more generals and more office generals, but only to a limit. We can train an infantryman in six months if he is paying attention, but it takes a quarter-century to grow a general. The top of the pyramid needs to be somewhat top heavy so that we can expand the base of the pyramid in times of need.

The generals and admirals that we have should wear fewer stars. The army averages about forty or so three-star generals at any one time. Of those, only four are in line warfighting positions, a few more in joint warfighting billets. Because we need more emphasis on warfighting and less on staff and headquarters concerns, this would be a good opportunity to pare back the number of generals we have and the number of stars they wear and stack the promotion deck in favor of warfighting and joint positions.

Two stars, by the way, is the highest permanent rank in any service. That is why when Maxwell Taylor was recalled to active duty in the Kennedy administration, he wore his uniform with only two stars on it and why MacArthur, complaining and petulant, had to take two stars off his uniform when he left the chief of staff position in Washington and traveled to the Philippines before World War II. All of our current three- and four-stars are temporary ranks that go with the job.[42] That is a contract for the rank, for the job, one assignment at a time. So that no one forgets the rules, each newly promoted or assigned three-star signs an undated letter of resignation at the start of each assignment. That letter resides in the service chief's office for the duration of the tour. If we begin to float the assignment rank back down toward the permanent rank, we can begin to reverse our current grade inflation.

Conservationists are of the view that everyone doesn't need to trek into the remote high forests of Africa to gape at mountain gorillas or traipse about China looking for pandas. It is enough, they think, to live in a world that can find a protected place for such grand animals.

That makes sense. It also isn't necessary for everyone in America to have some connection with the military or its values. It ought to be enough that the ideas of courage, integrity, and service to the nation exist in some protected place. There are other places where our values are honored, certainly, but at least for the first two centuries of our nation's history, our military has done well in safeguarding our values. Those that choose to be an active part of the military are welcome and the more people who make that choice the better. For those who don't, our values will be intact when the nation needs them.

Our senior officers are the stewards of those values. Many recruits now coming into the military no longer have the imprint of some of America's basic tenets.[43] The family and community and social structures that formerly hard-wired values into our young people now, in too many instances, are not there or are not working. The tradition-encrusted way of military thinking may be an obstacle to agile change, but it does work well in instilling and protecting values. People who serve the nation in uniform learn the deep-seated convictions of previous generations of Americans and, in turn, pass those convictions along to succeeding generations. Our military can be no better than the best of Americans, but we must be that best.

America and America's military share something even more basic than values. Freedom is America's purpose so the defense of freedom is our military's purpose. That freedom has been the engine for success in the American experiment in self-government and our senior officers are among its guarantors. That charge is a high honor and a task taken seriously by our military leaders, past and present.

George Washington's response to the cabal of Revolutionary officers who would challenge civilian authority was a foundation precedent. His conviction that the American Revolution had been fought for freedom, and that a challenge to civilian leaders challenged that freedom, began the fundamental tradition in our officer corps of civilian control of the military.

Andrew Jackson would fight at the drop of a hat, but he was most often going to war to challenge those who would challenge Americans' freedoms: the British in the American Revolution and the War of 1812, the Spanish in Florida. If Jackson's commitment to defending America's freedom had limits, he seems not to have reached those limits. As president, he was confronted with South Carolina's nullification of a federal tariff and an explicit threat of secession. Jackson said he would raise a militia army, march at its head to South Carolina and hang the first secessionist he found there from the nearest tree.[44] Jackson had led a militia force against the Indians and quieted the frontier, led the militia at New Orleans and defeated the British, led a militia army into Florida and claimed it from a failing Spanish colonial order. No one in South Carolina had reason to doubt Jackson's resolve and ability to do exactly what he said he would do. The threat of secession receded.

Ulysses Grant, more citizen than soldier, also understood that freedom is at America's center. He fought a to-the-death war to preserve the Union and, at Appomattox, offered a generous peace to the Confederate soldiers. In the morning, they were the enemy to be relentless pursued and brought to battle. By the afternoon, they were fellow citizens to be welcomed and saluted. Restoring their freedom restored the Union.

America's struggle in World War II was, at base, a contest between a democracy that governed its citizens by consent and the ambitions of dictators who ruled by conquest. George Marshall was the officer to lead that cause. He lived the values of the American officer corps, indeed, seemed to embody them in many ways. The leaders of Germany and Italy were not military officers but delighted in wearing field marshal uniforms. Marshall, who achieved five-star rank, was sworn in as chief of staff of the army wearing a civilian suit.

If the successful generals in our past were in uniform today, what would we want them to do? Washington, Jackson, Grant, Pershing, and Marshall all knew that America's warfighting strength lay with its citizen becoming soldiers. If these preeminent military leaders in America's history knew that, we should as well. It is a revealing comment on how the Pentagon operates today that the idea of citizen soldiers carrying the burden of our warfight is viewed as a radical idea. A bold general would look beyond the Pentagon budget and turf battles, beyond our Cold War mindset, and find that deeper source of our warfighting strength. There will be generals somewhere who will move their forces to the next level of warfighting capability. They should be American generals.

We want our generals to be of one mind with the presidents they serve. Every American victory has seen that happen: Washington deferring to, indeed sustaining, nascent civilian leadership in the American Revolution. Lincoln rooting through half a dozen generals in the Civil War before finding Grant. Wilson, ever the reluctant warrior, letting Pershing largely set America's war strategy in France in World War I. Roosevelt and Marshall in World War II. Where presidents and generals have failed to develop and share a sound strategy, victory has eluded us: Truman and MacArthur in Korea, Westmoreland and Johnson in Vietnam, George W. Bush and his generals for the first several years of the Iraq War.

It is a good thing for generals, within the closed councils of policy-making, to be disruptive. The officers who went along with presidents and secretaries of defense in the long years of Vietnam are nameless. Generals who will risk their careers on principle—the Ridgways and others—have better served the nation. We need a few generals who will kick over the traces.

CHAPTER 13:
Presidents

PRESIDENTS MUST LEAD: only in the presidency do civilian and military matters finally converge. The way ahead in rebuilding America's military might will require leadership from the oval office.

A leader to inform American presidents on such matters is Britain's World War II Prime Minister, Winston Churchill. Churchill, the first person to be named an honorary American by Congress, was half American by birth but altogether American by inclination. He had the habit of action. The grandson of a duke, Churchill was born into a world of wealth and privilege but supported himself precariously his entire life by his wit and his pen. Among the dozens of books and hundreds of articles he wrote, one is a perceptive volume on the American Civil War.[1]

Churchill knew war. He fought as a subaltern while Victoria still reigned, rode into close combat in Britain's last cavalry charge in 1898. While a member of the British cabinet in World War I, he learned to fly airplanes—in an era when the Wright brothers were still giving lessons—and advocated the wider use of air power before that was at all obvious. When he became prime minister in Great Britain's time of crisis in 1940, he kept the Ministry of Defense portfolio for himself, the first prime minister to do so, to assure that nothing came between him and his generals and admirals fighting the war.

Churchill was intuitive rather than logical.[2] In the 1930s, he saw Hitler and Nazism as evils that must be dealt with someday. While the rest of Britain's leadership found new ways to appease Hitler year after year, Churchill protested, loudly and often, from the political exile where his outspoken criticisms had landed him. His decade-long diatribe against Hitler and against Britain's slide to military unpreparedness proved to have been right. The others were wrong. Churchill heard voices others did not hear or at least did not heed. Most often, those voices spoke from moral fundamentals rather than from political expediency. This is a lesson American presidents should follow.

Our future presidents can also be informed on military matters by the Ronald Reagan presidency, although the lessons there lie inside a quandary. Things went well on Reagan's watch. Events accelerated toward a successful end to the four-decade Cold War. The economy was strong. After a dismal decade of Vietnam, Watergate, and malaise, Americans began to feel good about being Americans again. The quandary is that all of these things happened under a president who was widely portrayed as a not very bright actor who somehow found himself as president of the United States.

Perhaps Reagan was not as detached as was reported. In the years leading up to the presidency, he wrote in his private papers about his vision of what America could be.[3] What Reagan knew was fundamental to America and he knew it to his fingertips. Reagan understood that freedom is at the core of the American experience, that being on the right side of an issue is a source of long-term power, and that military strength is a decisive factor in deterring war or, if deterrence fails, in defending American interests.

Reagan did believe that the Soviet Union was evil. An empire that crushed the individual freedoms that Jefferson and the others had so eloquently bequeathed to Americans was, in Reagan's view, wrong. He would not accept compromise disguised as détente. His adamant opposition to the very idea of the Soviet Union, coupled with his support for America's military strength, precipitated the Soviet collapse and America's Cold War success. Reagan's core beliefs proved to be a framework for a successful presidency.

Reagan was altogether engaging. I met him when he made a presidential visit to Kentucky. Reagan walked down the steps of Air

Force One and began to greet the greeters. Events like that are rigorously arranged by protocol and there are people there to make sure the protocol is followed. The president worked his way down the line, genially but somewhat by rote. He got to the end of the line, saw my uniform and brightened visibly. When he grabbed my hand, I gave him my carefully prepared speech: "Welcome to Kentucky, Mr. President."

Reagan kept shaking my hand and told me about his World War II service. My First Cavalry Division combat patch has a horse on it and the president talked to me about horses. He talked about the pre–World War II cavalry. The civilian officials standing around were starting to give me questioning glances and I realized that the president of the United States had hold of my hand, and when he stopped talking, I was expected to say something.

When he quit talking, I responded: "Welcome to Kentucky, Mr. President." He seemed fine with that.

Future presidents can also learn from Theodore Roosevelt. Rudyard Kipling captured the tenor of his time when he said of Roosevelt and the start of the twentieth century that "the universe seemed to be spinning round and Theodore was the spinner."[4]

Roosevelt was the exuberant amateur: naturalist, cowboy, statesman, boxer, soldier. He was the spark of America at the dawn of what became known as the American century. He saw no limits to what he could do and no limits to what America could do. As assistant secretary of the navy, Roosevelt helped prod a reluctant McKinley administration into war with Spain. On an afternoon when the secretary of the navy was out of the office, Roosevelt sent a flurry of messages to the fleet to get ready to go to war. Roosevelt then resigned to go fight the war he had helped start. McKinley and Congress authorized volunteer cavalry regiments of frontiersmen called cowboy cavalry. That phrase had no plausible military meaning, but it clearly included Roosevelt somehow. Colonel Leonard Wood, the secretary of war's physician, was made colonel of a regiment, with Roosevelt as lieutenant colonel.

Roosevelt recruited his regiment from a mix of Ivy Leaguers and rough westerners.[5] The heroic ineptitude of the army's deployment to Cuba gave Roosevelt a lifelong disdain for War Department bureaucrats. In Cuba, now in command of the regiment, Roosevelt found a battle. He led the attack up the San Juan heights with enthusiasm, was the only mounted soldier in the charge, and carried his regiment with him. In a very full life, that was his defining moment, what he ever after referred to as his crowded hour.[6]

Roosevelt became a national hero. Six months after his battle in Cuba, he was elected governor of New York. Twelve months later, he was vice president and six months after that, upon McKinley's assassination in 1901, Roosevelt became the youngest man ever to be president. Not since Lincoln had there been such an energetic leader in the White House. Roosevelt had a knack for getting his way. He took on the trusts, the oil and railroad moguls. Roosevelt the naturalist and hunter made conservation and national parks part of the American agenda.

A sense of Roosevelt and his America was captured in the building of the Panama Canal. For centuries, people dreamed of a waterway across the narrow isthmus of Central America, a link between two oceans when oceans were the only means of global travel. The French tried and failed, squandering their national pride and nearly wrecking their economy in the pestilent jungles and mountain gorges of Panama.

When Theodore Roosevelt set his mind to it, there would be a canal, but it would not be easy. First there were the recalcitrant Colombians, who declined to sell the rights to build the canal on terms that Roosevelt deemed fair. So Roosevelt became midwife to a revolution and a new country—the former Colombian province of Panama—around his canal. The London papers called it land piracy. Roosevelt took no notice. There was talk of a neutral canal. Roosevelt put sixteen-inch guns at the entrances to the canal to dispel any doubts as to whose canal it was.[7]

Then there was the Herculean task of engineering and excavating the canal. Roosevelt sent in a railroad man who could make the dirt fly. Malaria decimated the work force. Roosevelt sent in army doctors to beat the disease.[8] Roosevelt saw the canal not just as a pathway between two oceans but as a pathway for America to a position of world influence.

Along with his canal, Roosevelt wanted warships. Britannia ruled the waves then and capital ships were very much the measure of a nation's power and prestige. Roosevelt would see that America had its fair share. When the new American fleet was of a respectable size, Roosevelt announced an around-the-world cruise to show the American flag. Congress refused to appropriate the funds. Roosevelt ordered the fleet to sea and swore that they would sail as far as their fuel lasted and then drop anchor until Congress came up with the funds to get them home. Congress did.[9]

Roosevelt's boldness would be a breath of fresh air in what now passes for presidential leadership. Any list of enduring American accomplishments attributable to presidential vision would surely include Roosevelt's canal. As it would Eisenhower's interstate highway system and John Kennedy's manned space flight to the moon. The last half-century has produced no obvious additions to such a list.

These lessons from Churchill and Reagan and Roosevelt are what generals want presidents to know: where the military fits into the larger American purpose. To chart a clear course, not merely chase events and domestic political considerations. To meet a standard of our officer corps: do the right thing for the right reasons. To lead with vision and tenacity and to pick the right senior officers and then have confidence in their ability. Those are high standards for presidents, but the costs of failure are grievous when America goes to war.

There is also a lesson in the fact that generals who win wars have a way of becoming president. George Washington came to personify the American Revolution to Americans of his era and could be trusted as a steward of their freedoms. Andrew Jackson could be relied upon as a staunch defender of the still forming United States. Zachary Taylor had few discernable qualifications for the presidency other than his Mexican War triumphs. Grant emerged from the cataclysm of the Civil War as the savior of the Union. Eisenhower stepped to the cusp of a presidential nomination without anyone knowing with certainty his political party allegiance.[10]

Presidential elections are the definitive expression of America's trust. That the presidency has gone so often to generals in different eras reflects a strong bond between Americans and their army. Leaders honed in the hard test of war can be assumed to have our commonly held values in great measure. Presidents don't need to pretend to be generals. Franklin Roosevelt nurtured and used George Marshall's generalship to his ends and to the nation's advantage. In the Roosevelt/Marshall partnership, Roosevelt was far and away the senior partner. A good president can appropriate a good general.

In the American way of war, presidents and generals must understand one another. In World War II, Franklin Roosevelt and General Marshall directed an army and an army air force of over eight million men and women. That huge force was fighting in simultaneous campaigns in nine separate theaters of war.[11] The political and diplomatic challenges were formidable: America had to coax concerted action from thirty allied nations, each of which had its own goals and its own ideas about how the war should be conducted. The war was being fought for the most fundamental of reasons—the freedom of America and its allies.

Roosevelt and Marshall fought this complex and global war without a national security adviser, without a national security council, without a White House staff of any appreciable size, without a secretary of defense and without the gaggle of deputy secretaries and undersecretaries and deputy undersecretaries and assistant secretaries and deputy assistant secretaries that now fill and overfill the policymaking landscape in Washington. Roosevelt and Marshall fought and won a world war by meeting, face to face, frequently and regularly. They discussed issues and made decisions and then the chiefs of the army and the navy and the army air forces left the room and implemented those decisions. That was by Roosevelt's choice. When Marshall was reorganizing the army just after Pearl Harbor, Roosevelt gave the secretary of war specific guidance to "make it very clear that the commander in chief exercises his command function in relation to strategy, tactics and operations directly through the army chief of staff."[12]

The war stretched quite literally around the world. The campaigns were immensely complex. The stakes were truly dire. But the decision making to deal with all that was straightforward. Roosevelt and Marshall came to be of one mind about how to fight the war. Even presidents as good as Roosevelt need the counsel of their generals and admirals. The strategic insight that our senior flag officers bring with them to work every day should be a part of the defense decisions that presidents must make.

Why we go to war matters. In Korea, we deployed military forces to aid an ally that had been invaded and our military forces restored the prewar border. Korea came to be viewed as a stalemate. Our forces still defend the border between South Korea and North Korea more than a half-century after the war there ended. In Desert Storm, we deployed military forces to aid an ally that had been invaded and restored the prewar border. That came to be viewed as a decisive victory. Both views are correct. The difference is in why we went to war. In Korea, we were opposing what we thought was a monolithic world communist aggression: what happened on the ground in Korea could not determine success or failure in that strategy. In Desert Storm, we were answering aggression to deter further aggression: what happened on the ground in Kuwait determined success or failure. That is an easy call to make with the benefit of hindsight, a very hard call to make if you are a president peering into a murky future. Strategic insight from generals will help.

How we go to war matters. We went to war in Vietnam for the same reason we went to war in Korea: to resist communist aggression. But in Vietnam, we fielded a conventional war response to meet an insurgent threat. Success or failure in Vietnam was determined by things other than America's conventional arms: the legitimacy of the government of South Vietnam, the allegiance of the people of South Vietnam to the competing forms of government, and their willingness to fight to defend their choice. Many of the same challenges arose in the Iraq War. These are painfully hard issues for any president to get right and insight from generals will help.

Civilians determine the kind of counsel they get. A long-serving secretary of defense who makes flag officer promotions a matter of loyalty to a given presidential administration will eventually get the counsel he wants. Secretary Rumsfeld did just that in the years before we went to war in Iraq. Go-to-war decisions are better made if secretaries of defense and presidents seek contentious counsel and contentious counselors.

One of the values that is commonplace in the military and that seems scarce elsewhere in Washington is loyalty. People in the military say that loyalty works both ways, both up and down the chain of command. That should apply to presidents as well. When a recent JCS chairman—Marine Gen. Peter Pace—successfully completed his first two-year term, the White House declined to nominate him for the customary second two years because they did not want to undergo the scrutiny of their Iraq War policy that Senate confirmation for the reappointment would entail. At his retirement ceremony, General Pace closed his remarks by recounting a promise he made to himself on behalf of the young marines in his platoon who were killed in Vietnam. That promise was to stay in uniform and try to do the best he could for the country in such a way as to pay respect to the sacrifices they had made. Pace did that for nearly forty years. After the retirement ceremony, he went to the Vietnam Memorial where the names of those killed in the war are etched in the black marble wall. He left three cards there, each with the name of a marine who died in his platoon in Vietnam. Pinned to each card was a set of four-star insignia and the words: "These are yours—not mine."[13] Loyalty between presidents and generals—loyalty in both directions—will make presidents better presidents and generals better generals.

Our future leaders—presidents and secretaries of defense and flag officers—must reconnect presidents with their senior officers. Presidents have to lead, secretaries of defense must set policy, and generals and admirals have to offer independent and hard-edged counsel. Defense decisions, particularly go-to-war decisions, will always be difficult, but our chances of making the right decision improve dramatically if direct, forceful counsel from generals and admirals is a part of final defense decision making. The surest way to prevent strategic insight from reaching presidents is to bureaucratically isolate presidents from their generals or to co-opt senior flag officers into civilian decision making and forfeit their independent advice. To our detriment, that is precisely what we have done.

Generals can still win wars. One very nearly did in Vietnam.

In the spring of 1972, America faced a military crisis. In what came to be known as the Easter Offensive, the North Vietnamese tried to overwhelm the dwindling American forces in Vietnam and the questionable combat power of the resuscitated Army of the Republic of Vietnam. The North Vietnamese began a conventional force invasion of South Vietnam. This was not insurgency. This was tanks and infantry and artillery attacking.[14]

The American commander in Vietnam was the short, brusque armor branch officer Creighton Abrams. He had been a battalion commander for Patton in World War II and had commanded the lead battalion for the relief of Bastogne.[15] Four-star generals are expected to be a mix of diplomat and soldier: if there was a diplomatic part of Abrams, it was not overly developed.

In mid-1968, Abrams assumed command in Vietnam from General Westmoreland and changed the American strategy there. Body counts became less important than village security, how well the military forces of South Vietnam performed became more important than tons of bombs dropped by American bombers. The strategic goal became less killing North Vietnamese and more garnering the political allegiance of the South Vietnamese for their government.[16] By 1972, it was working.[17]

The Easter Offensive of that year also became a crisis in the White House. America was pursuing a policy called Vietnamization, by which the United States was somehow to pass title to the war to the South Vietnamese. The North Vietnamese attack threatened the credibility of that policy. More important in a presidential election year, the North Vietnamese attack also threatened the political well-being of the sitting president. Such a threat galvanizes a White House staff like nothing else.

The White House peppered Abrams with a flurry of questions and suggestions. Abrams stayed the course and his years of emphasis on pacification in the countryside and on improving the capability of the armed forces of South Vietnam proved successful. But the Abrams strategy was too little, too late. The American public's tolerance for war in Vietnam was gone. The withdrawal of American forces continued and American promises of ongoing equipment, financial aid, and combat air support that were made as we withdrew were later rescinded by Congress. The next North Vietnamese conventional invasion in 1975 succeeded.

In the end, it is presidents who must lead. That places an enormous burden on presidents, and it is a burden we are not meeting. Presidents formerly governed between campaigns, now they govern by campaigning: it has somehow become acceptable for reelection to take precedence over the merits of defense issues. The incessantly partisan atmosphere in Washington now taints defense policymaking. Matters of war and peace, of victory and defeat, are more important than any given politician's future, more important than any given political party's well-being. We must restore defense to the all but extinct category of bipartisan issues.

A president, any president, can go far toward fixing the flaws in our current defense. A president can enforce a seriously joint approach to the warfight by ordering it and then periodically checking on his generals' progress. A president can reinvolve senior officers in final defense decision making simply by calling them to the White House and doing so. And then doing so again. Any president can have independent counsel by demanding it. These steps take no legislation, they take only leadership and good sense.

A harder task—and it also falls to presidents—is to lead the American public to the understanding that defense is every citizen's obligation. National service will be described as a disguised military draft—and, in some measure, it is—but all Americans must share the burden when America goes to war. It strikes a discordant note to us today to be reminded that draftees into the Union Army in the Civil War could avoid service by paying a cash bonus to a substitute. Theodore Roosevelt was perhaps somewhere between embarrassed and ashamed that his beloved and admired father had done just that. We should today be somewhere between embarrassed and ashamed that we are now doing the same thing: defense of the nation is now more a budget issue than a matter of shared obligation among all Americans. That is adequate for between war missions but it will not work for major wars.

Nor is it sufficient to assume that Americans can take up arms for our next major war because they have in previous eras. Our past victories have become clouded in a haze of patriotism and legend. The American Revolution, the Civil War, and both world wars could well have been lost. Victory was much less certain at the time than history has made it appear. It was our citizens' willingness to become soldiers that brought victory. It will be our citizens' willingness to become soldiers that will bring future victories. Presidents must look to and strengthen the bond between our citizens and our soldiers before war comes again.

There will be wars in our future and America will need presidents and generals who understand that military preparedness is the best chance for peace or, if peace fails, the best chance for victory. That is not militarism and it is not an open checkbook for military expenditures. But it is developing a credible defense strategy and then being able to raise the forces that can execute that strategy. It is our baseline strengths—our economy, the connection between America and its military, the legitimacy of a war decision, and the trust Americans have in their leaders—that are the real source of America's military might. An American military joined to the American people and committed to defending freedom is our best chance for deterring war and the best chance for winning wars we cannot deter.

Presidents, like generals, must lead from the front. Theodore Roosevelt showed that spirit before he was president when he led that charge at the San Juan heights, showed it exuberantly in the White House, and showed it again when he volunteered to raise and lead a division of Rough Riders in World War I after leaving the presidency.[18] Bold leaders will make mistakes. As a colleague said of Churchill, "Winston was often right, but when he was wrong, well, my God."[19] Occasional mistakes are better than timidity and indecision. A cautious bureaucracy will neither keep the peace nor win wars.

The presidential leadership that we must have will come from presidents who put defense decisions ahead of their own political concerns. Presidents are key in renewing America's military might, but the real source of the needed changes lies with the American public. It is our country, our government, and they are our wars. When enough Americans understand and accept that ownership, presidents will respond.

CHAPTER 14:
Soldiers

OUR ARMY AND THE OFFICERS AND SOLDIERS IN IT are defined by our values. When our values are honored, we can win battles and wars. When they are not, victory is unlikely. A battle where our values were self-evident happened in the Vietnam War in the first major fight between American combat units and the North Vietnamese Army.

That battle took place in the Ia Drang, a remote river valley in the Central Highlands of Vietnam. The North Vietnamese Army purpose in the Ia Drang was ambitious: defeat the foreign army and then drive across the narrow waist of Vietnam, cutting the country in half. The North Vietnamese, just several miles from their sanctuary across the border in Cambodia, picked the terrain they wanted to fight, prepared positions, stockpiled supplies, and waited.[1]

The Americans sent their first team to the fight, the 1st Air Cavalry Division. The 1st Cav was equipped and trained for this very kind of battle. Two years before, the U.S. Army decided to capture the mobility of helicopters and bring that capability to wars like Vietnam. For those two years, the 1st Cav trained in helicopter assaults, air reconnaissance, and helicopter gunship support. When Lyndon Johnson announced to a surprised America in July 1965, that he was sending American forces into combat in Vietnam, what he announced was that he was sending the 1st Air Cavalry Division to the war.

The fight at Ia Drang began when the 1st battalion of the 7th Cavalry, an infantry battalion, air assaulted into a small clearing in the jungle. Vietnam was the second war for the battalion commander, Lt. Col. Hal Moore, who had been a combat infantryman in Korea. Some of his other officers had served in Korea as well and some of his senior non-commissioned officers were on their third war: World War II, Korea, and now Vietnam.

Their soldiers were mostly draftees but came to the war in a very different way from those that would follow. Much of this battalion, indeed much of the entire division, had the old army advantage of time. They came as units, by and large, not as individual replacements. Many had trained together, the leaders knew their soldiers and the soldiers their leaders. They had built the unit cohesion that allows soldiers to succeed in combat.

There was nothing about the initial assault into the Ia Drang to indicate that this battle would become famous. Moore was on the lead helicopter to touch down. Because of the size of the landing zone, he could only bring in eight helicopters at a time. Moore had sixteen helicopters assigned to him that day, so he could land something less than a full infantry company—of his four-company battalion—in a series of assault landings. Those landings began at mid-morning and would take several hours to get the entire battalion on the ground.

Each Huey helicopter held eight or nine soldiers, an infantry squad led by a sergeant. As soon as the helicopters touched down, the squads and platoons assembled and moved to secure a portion of the perimeter of the landing zone (LZ). That LZ was the lifeline for the battle and for the soldiers fighting it. More troops, ammunition, water, and medical supplies would come in through the LZ. The wounded and the dead would leave through it. Protecting the LZ was protecting the combat power to win the fight. At Dien Bien Phu, the French lost their air field, in effect, lost their LZ.

With an infantryman's eye for terrain, Moore began securing the north and west sides of the circular LZ. As the perimeter was being manned, he sent forces forward to intercept any enemy attack as far from the LZ as possible. That is how and where the battle began. Moore's advancing units ran into a much larger enemy force moving toward the LZ.

The basic infantry tactic in the U.S. Army is fire and maneuver. A squad will stay in position and fire at the enemy while another squad attacks to the right or left looking for an unprotected flank of the enemy force. Flank attacks work because the entire attacking force can fire at just one end of the enemy line, an overwhelming advantage in firepower.

The company Moore sent forward had two platoons advancing, one beside the other. When one platoon was pinned down by heavy fire, the other maneuvered to find an open flank. In the confusion and fear of combat, units get lost. One of Moore's platoons attacked too far forward and was cut off by the much more numerous North Vietnamese Army (NVA). That platoon's officer was killed and a junior sergeant took charge. They became a lost platoon, surrounded and under heavy fire.

Moore kept bringing in forces through the fire-swept LZ. He extended his perimeter defense farther along the west and then around to the south. When it became clear that something important was happening in the Ia Drang, units from other battalions in the Cav were flown in and placed under Moore's command. Night came and the NVA attacks continued. The 1st Cav had placed twelve artillery pieces at a forward fire support base several miles away. Those guns fired thousands of rounds that night to help hold the perimeter. Twelve more guns were added in the morning. Air force strikes and helicopter gunships ringed the battalion's position day and night with supporting fires, but the NVA were often too near the American perimeter for artillery or air support to be used: this was a close in infantry fight, in some cases literally hand to hand.

Dawn of the second day found the 1st battalion of the 7th Cav still there, its units intact and fighting, junior leaders stepping in for more senior leaders who were killed or badly wounded. The battalion attacked and recovered their beleaguered lost platoon.

Moore was busy. He placed and maneuvered his forces as they flew in, coordinated artillery and air strikes where he could, brought in supplies, and evacuated wounded through the LZ. He tried to anticipate the NVA's next moves, pieced together a battalion reserve, and deployed it at critical times and places. Moore also dealt with his higher headquarters, telling Saigon that he could not leave his battalion to go brief them on the still unfolding battle.

At last light of the second day of the battle, Moore and his senior non-commissioned officer, Sergeant Major Basil Plumley, made their way around the entire perimeter of the LZ. They checked the positioning of the units, making sure there were no gaps in their line. They checked the placement of their machine guns and mortars. Moore could see which of his officers and sergeants were still alive, which were still able to lead and fight. He could look into the eyes of his soldiers and take their measure. They, importantly, could see him. Troops fight best when they see their leaders and know their leaders know their business.

Moore's battalion, reinforced by elements of two other Cav battalions, fought a much larger NVA force for three days and two nights of nearly continuous combat. Moore's maneuvering of forces on the ground, his use of supporting fires, and his hands-on control were the keys to winning the battle. Moore's battalion and its attached units lost 79 killed and 121 wounded. The NVA lost 634 killed in the close in fight and another estimated 1,215 killed or wounded by artillery and air strikes.[2] This draftee army, well led, proved that they could fight as well as any Americans ever had. Moore was on the last helicopter taking his battalion out of the Ia Drang.

Our values worked. Battle leaders were capable and present. Soldiers were motivated and courageous. Americans fight well for a mix of reasons. At the Ia Drang, leadership, training, and unit cohesion won a tough fight. Those assets are achievable in any era.

✵ ✵ ✵ ✵

In the early morning hours of March 16, 1968, as part of another battalion air assault, two infantry companies loaded their helicopters at a firebase in Quang Ngai province in Central Vietnam. A third company was already on the ground in a blocking position. The objective was a series of Viet Cong–controlled villages on the coast of the South China Sea. The villages were called Pinkville by the Americans because of some obscure cartographer's choice of map colors. The Vietnamese called the villages Son My, the hamlet where the assault was to take place, Thuan Yen. It has passed into history as My Lai.

Charlie Company of Task Force Baker of the Americal Division would lead the assault. A five-minute artillery barrage preceded their landing, gunships fired along the edge of the LZ. Charlie Company's first platoon, under the command of 2nd Lt. William Calley, landed at 7:30 in the morning and moved west to east through the village. Second Platoon on its left, commanded by 2nd Lt. Stephen Brooks, was to take a parallel track.

Charlie Company was on a search and destroy mission. That meant that it could engage any enemy force it found, detain civilians that were actively supporting the enemy, and destroy military supplies captured. Search and destroy was a valid tactic, but there is no American tactic for what happened at My Lai.

The Americans were not fired on during their landing. Calley's platoon moved into the village, shooting and bayoneting fleeing civilians and rounded up women and children and old men: then they began shooting the groups of unarmed civilians. When his machine gunner hesitated, Calley took the machine gun himself and killed a group of about twenty Vietnamese. He did that twice more that morning and personally killed perhaps as many as seventy civilians. To their left, 2nd Platoon killed between fifty and a hundred unarmed civilians and gang-raped two women. Between the two units, the best American estimate is that 347 unarmed civilians were killed at My Lai.[3]

Some soldiers refused to participate. One shot himself in the foot to get airlifted out of the area. An American helicopter pilot landed his observation helicopter between Calley's men and a dozen frightened civilians. He left his aircraft to rescue the civilians, telling his door gunner to shoot Calley's men if they tried to interfere.

Rumors about the event began to spread, and a soldier wrote a letter to senior officials in Washington. The army initially dragged its feet but then woke up to the fact that something despicable had happened at My Lai. There were investigations and inquiries and courts-martial. The end result was that no one except Calley was convicted. A court-martial found him guilty and sentenced him to life in prison. That sentence was reduced to twenty years by the court martial review authority, the general officer on whose authority the court-martial was conducted, and then reduced to ten years by the secretary of the army. Calley served a short sentence, much of it under house arrest in comfortable government quarters at Ft. Benning. He was paroled by President Nixon.[4]

Calley and the others at My Lai broke innumerable laws and regulations and were subject to any number of Uniform Code of Military Justice sanctions, all of which came to next to nothing. American soldiers don't behave well or badly in combat because of regulations. They do well or badly because of our values and our leadership. Ours is an army of values. Service to the nation ranks high. Courage, both physical and moral, is a big part of what our people in uniform do. Integrity matters. These same values have been the mainstay of our military since the nation was founded. They change little, and that slowly. Calley abandoned those values or more likely never understood them.

Our values and our traditions are enforced and shaped and passed on by our officer corps. The military is an insular society: there is a kind of monasticism at work here. When our leaders keep faith with our values—from the newest lieutenant or junior sergeant to the most senior general—our military works. When they don't, it doesn't.

The army that withdrew from Vietnam was a very different army from the one that went there, very different from the soldiers of the 1st Cav that fought at the Ia Drang Valley. Our army after 1966 went to war one scared eighteen-year-old at a time. That individual replacement system assured that our young and green soldiers were dropped into combat without the unit cohesion that sustains soldiers in war. They did not know their leaders, by and large, and what they did know often did not fill them with confidence. As a result, the army in Vietnam struggled to maintain its values. My Lai was an aberration, but it happened. My Lai occurred because our soldiers went to war without our core values intact and without the leaders in place to enforce those values.

General Westmoreland became a cardboard caricature for the anti-war movement during the Vietnam War and those images have followed him into history. He must accept responsibility for the merit—or lack of merit—of his strategy on the ground there, but he deserves a better reputation for his integrity. It was Westmoreland's decision to forthrightly investigate the then only rumored incident at My Lai. The civilian leadership in the Pentagon, and probably the White House staff, resisted his efforts. Westmoreland had to threaten to go directly to the president, with an implicit threat of going public, to launch the Peers Commission, the definitive account of what happened at My Lai that led to what official action there was.[5]

I have been to My Lai. My army did this and I ought to have the character to stand on the ground where it happened. Generals learn as much from our failures, as painful as they are, as from our flag waving victories. Our values were tested at the Ia Drang and prevailed. Our values were tested at My Lai and failed.

Why American soldiers fight is hard to understand and even harder to explain. But with the right leadership, in the right situation, they do. For clarity, the American Civil War shows soldiers in an uncluttered light in a simpler time.

Wilbur Fisk was a private in E Company of the 2nd Vermont Volunteer Regiment. E Company was recruited in his hometown of Tunbridge, Vermont, at the beginning of the war. He started and ended the war as a private. That does not speak to a lack of ambition as much as to his sense of place and role: Fisk wrote in his diary that "Here I have to lug a knapsack on every march, fight in every battle and do not claim any exemption from the roughest in the crowd. After all I shouldn't like the idea of being cheated out of the name of having been in these battles and I take a sort of pride in doing a common soldier's duty."[6]

Fisk understood that it is the privates in any army who do the vast majority of the fighting. Generals can get their armies to the right place and at the right time, colonels and majors and captains can lead and direct the battle but it is the privates who fight. Fisk had a musket-level view of the war.

And like almost all privates, he spent a large part of his time and concern trying to stay alive and, when not being shot at, staying comfortable. When it rained, he was wet. During the winter he was cold and during the summer he was hot. His days were defined by what rations he was given or could scrounge, if he marched and how far he marched, and how close his Army of the Potomac was to the enemy. Fisk did the things as a private soldier then that privates still do: stand guard, pine for home, and wonder at the imbecility of higher headquarters.

Fisk was a perceptive witness to the events around him and wrote with clarity and an eye for detail. Over the course of the war and with conscious regularity, he wrote one hundred letters to the editor of the *Montpelier Green Mountain Freeman*. These letters were periodic reports of what was happening in the part of the war that Fisk could see. He also made nearly daily entries in his diary. Other soldiers wrote letters, many kept diaries. Fisk did it well and he is a window on his war. Largely self-educated, he could turn a phrase. Rations were "Meat and bread or, for a change, bread and meat . . . any intelligent pig possessing the least spark of pride would have considered it a pure insult to put them into his swill."[7] When President Lincoln reviewed his regiment, Fisk described him as "looking thin and careworn."[8] To describe his regiment's resolve in an action: "There was no skedaddling to the rear."[9]

One of the first things Fisk experienced as a soldier was picket duty, standing guard around a camp or facing the enemy force. Early in the war, on picket duty within walking distance of Washington, Fisk filled the night hours of guard duty with musing that his picket line was the limit of the American Union: in front of him lay only darkness and rebellion, behind him lay what was left of America. He was right.

Fisk described his fellow privates as a broad range of young men: some contemplative, others boisterous and profane. The best he saw as committed to suppressing the rebellion. And he saw the best of the Army of the Potomac as being the regiments or brigades from Vermont. He was of the firm opinion that when a general needed a tough and important job done, he would be well served by having a Vermont unit do it. The fact that other soldiers held the same opinion about their states either didn't occur to Fisk or was dismissed as obviously wrong.

Fisk was fighting to preserve the Union. He and the others called the Confederates "secesh," a dismissive term for secessionist. They were the adversary but not, as later came to be the practice, a demonized enemy. On picket duty at Fredericksburg, Fisk and the other Union soldiers had many conversations with the Confederates just across the river. They exchanged newspapers and mail. Fisk was surprised how similar their views on the war were to his own. He decided it was a pity to have to shoot such good fellows. He also decided that if it was left to privates to run the war, there would very soon be no war.

At Fredericksburg, while much of the Army of the Potomac was sacrificing itself in front of the stonewall at Marye's Heights, Fisk and the Sixth Corps made better progress to the right of Lee's line. The 2nd Vermont Regiment was to follow the 26th New Jersey and attack the Confederate position. The 26th soldiers took to ground or were killed by a withering fire. The 2nd Vermont slipped to the right and continued the attack. In a stiff fight, they took their part of the hill for a time. A man next to Fisk was shot and would die in minutes. Told he was dying and ask if he had any last words, the wounded soldier said: "Tell them I was a good soldier."[10] Certainly he was.

At Gettysburg, Fisk's regiment was not in the hard parts of the fight. After the battle, in the desultory Union pursuit of Lee as the Confederates withdrew, Fisk and the 2nd Vermont went past the rock strewn defile known as Devil's Den. Here is his description of what he saw there:

> Over this forbidding ground, the rebels had made several fruitless charges, and many of their men, and ours, fell here to rise no more. . . . The rebel dead and ours lay thickly together, their thirst for blood forever quenched. Their bodies were swollen, black and hideously unnatural. Their eyes glared from their sockets, their tongues protruded from mouths, and in almost every case, clots of blood and mangled flesh showed how they had died, and rendered a sight ghastly beyond description.[11]

When Grant took command of the Union armies, the campaign against Lee became relentless. At the Wilderness battle, Fisk and the 2nd Vermont fought well the first day, advancing into a heavy enemy fire and driving the Confederates back. On the second day of the battle, they advanced again. The unit on their left collapsed, and the 2nd Vermont retreated at the run. When they got to the rear, Fisk kept going. He found some food and then found his regiment. On the third day of the battle, the 2nd Vermont was ordered forward yet again. Fisk didn't want to go but more did not want to "act the coward." When one of his fellow soldiers said "Come on boys," Fisk wasn't going to be left behind: "I clinched my musket and pushed ahead, determined to die if die I must, in my place and like a man."[12]

At Spotsylvania, Fisk was in what has often been described as the deadliest part of any battle of the war: the Bloody Angle. Fisk recounted in is his diary: "We charged square up to the breastworks and had a regular hand to hand fight all day. The rebs were on one side of the rifle pit and breastworks and we on the other. The fight was terribly destructive. Almost every shot took effect. Our company had five killed and we think six. The next morning the rebels left. Their pit was full of dead men. It was a horrid sight on either side of the breastwork."[13]

Fisk describes Cold Harbor in his diary: "The rebs poured a terrible fire into us of grape and canister besides a line of rifle pits with infantry that rained their bullets upon us in a perfect shower." Of the littered battlefield after they retreated back to where they started: "I picked up a half tent and all the hard tack I wanted."[14]

Second Wilderness, Spotsylvania, and Cold Harbor were hard fought battles. Grant said he was going to hammer Lee until his army was no more. Joshua Lawrence Chamberlain wrote at the time that it was a sound strategy but "hard on the hammer."[15] Fisk would have agreed.

The Army of the Potomac's resolve to fight the war was put to the test in Lincoln's bid for reelection. The dimensions of an American Civil War, unseen and probably not foreseeable at the onset of the conflict, had become painfully apparent. The loss of life was staggering. In today's America, a comparable number of dead would be five million.[16] General George McClellan, the twice sacked commander of the Army of the Potomac, was running as the Democratic peace candidate to oppose Lincoln and to oppose the war. He was still and would always be beloved by that army.

The vote of the Union soldiers was telling. Absentee ballots have become commonplace now but they were invented then to allow Union soldiers to vote in this presidential election. The people bearing the cost of the war, Private Fisk and the others, voted four to one for Lincoln and to continue the war. They viewed any peace settlement that allowed the Confederacy to remain in existence on any terms as unacceptable and as a betrayal of the sacrifices they had made.

Fisk appears extraordinary only if you don't know infantry privates. America has had soldiers of resilience and resolve in all of our wars and we still have them in our army today.

PART III
BEDROCK

CHAPTER 15

The Next War

THE PENTAGON TRIES VERY HARD TO FATHOM THE FUTURE, to identify threats that are coming over the horizon so that the United States can develop the capabilities to respond to those threats. Here is how the Pentagon plans to fight our next war.

Our current war planning process is scenario-driven. Each of the warfighting combatant commanders develops a war plan for his theater, his threat, and his terrain based on the anticipated actions of our potential adversaries.[1] The services then recruit, train, and equip the forces to fight those plans. The obvious shortfall in the process is that wars seldom follow war plans. Wars start in the wrong place at unexpected times and in unanticipated ways. But an off-target plan to start from is better than no plan at all.

Our current war plans are bounded by the basic decisions we have already made:

• We are a power projection force. We have to transport our forces to some distant part of the world and then begin the fight.

• We are a joint force. We will fight with land, air, and naval forces combining their combat power.

• We are a high-tech force. Precision maneuver and precision munitions beat human wave assaults every time.

Our war plans have a schedule. Airplanes are fast so air power gets there first. The navy and their carrier battle groups come early and with their own support assets onboard or afloat. When they arrive, they are ready to start the war. Land-based air also brings much of their support package with them. Both types of air power are there in a matter of days and weeks. Land power is usually the decisive force, but it takes longer to get there. We can move the troops by air but almost all of their equipment must come by sea. The Pentagon has pre-positioned a brigade set here and there and the marines maintain a brigade's worth of equipment afloat. That helps, but it is not a sustained warfighting force. Land power now takes something on the order of six months or longer to get in the fight.

The idea is that the forces deployed early will stabilize and contain the conflict. That essentially means hold some ground, airfields, or seaports so the rest of the force can flow into theater. As major forces get there, they will take the offensive and bring the battle to the enemy.

That is the plan—it will not work. Just as our force fits the budget we have rather than budgeting for the force we need, our war plans fit the force we have rather than planning for the force we will need. One of the reasons we are missing the mark is that war plans try to predict the future and, however smart or well intentioned our war planners are, predicting the future is hard. A longer time frame helps. The outlines of our next most likely war are contained in the causes and events of our past wars.

The American Revolution was fought by colonists seeking the freedom to have their own government to support their own ends. We took from that formative experience a deeply rooted tradition of fighting our wars with citizen soldiers and maintaining a modest standing army between wars. That was not a budget decision, it was who we were and is who we are. Each of our wars through World War II confirmed that approach.

The War of 1812 was an aftershock of the American Revolution: Britain did not take American sovereignty seriously but the newly independent Americans assuredly did. We still do. Andrew Jackson's improbable victory at New Orleans, like George Washington's strategic leadership in the American Revolution, showed that in the American way of war, general officer leadership matters a great deal. We do not fight our wars by committee.

The Mexican War was America expanding at the expense of Mexico and the European colonial powers who still had ambitions in the Americas. The United States had already dramatically increased its size by acquiring the vast Mississippi River watershed in the Louisiana Purchase and by inducing a weakened Spain to sell Florida. The Mexican War was another step along the path of becoming a continental power, stretching from one ocean to the other.

The Civil War was a resolution of the issues that defied agreement at the Constitutional Convention in Philadelphia in 1787: the authority of the federal government and who could be a citizen. Those questions were resolved with finality in battle. The Southern states saw the Union as a threat to their freedom, while the Northern states saw the Union as the source of theirs. In either case, it was a war about freedom.

The Spanish-American War saw America asserting its ambition to be a world power. It was a short war of little moment but a war that made America—at least for a time—a colonial power.

World War I was America's first war as a world power. The war arose from festering divisions among European nations and heroically inept statecraft. Germany's heavy-handed naval strategy of sinking American ships on the high seas pulled a reluctant America into this European war. The fresh American divisions proved to be the balance for the Allied victory.

World War II found America defending its freedom and sovereignty against the aggression of Germany and Japan. America's home front and industrial base were mobilized and were critical to our success. Victory in World War II made the United States a superpower.

What we still call the Cold War was not in fact a war but rather a strategic standoff with the Soviet Union. The Cold War was a victory of deterrence: Western ideals and the private market economies they allow eventually prevailed.

Korea was a rush to war in response to the invasion of non-Communist South Korea by Communist North Korea. We started the war there tactically unprepared and with the president and his commanding general pursuing conflicting strategies. In time, we found the leadership and the forces to restore the prewar border, but avoiding defeat in this limited war was as close to victory as we were likely to come.

Vietnam was a continuation of the Cold War concept of opposing Communist aggression but in slow motion: the attack by communist North Vietnam against non-Communist South Vietnam was an incremental insurgency. America's failure in Vietnam was more the result of flawed policymaking—attributable to both presidents and generals—than of battlefield setbacks.

Desert Storm was a response to outright aggression. Iraq's Army was expelled from Kuwait with wide international support and decisive military action. America and its Coalition partners went to war to check the kind of aggression that leads to wider wars. Public support for a successful one-hundred-hour war is obviously more easily garnered than public support for wars that last years and have no clear end point.

The Iraq War was an elective war the United States chose to start to pre-empt a perceived threat from Iraq's use of weapons of mass destruction. That cause for war proved to be unfounded. A strategy and a force designed for a short our-army-against-their-army war in fact confronted what turned out to be a long-term counterinsurgency.

There are clear trends in America's wars, and those trends will help us see at least the outlines of our next war.

The United States went from being militarily and economically weak in the American Revolution and in the War of 1812, to parity with competing powers in World War I and World War II, and on to tactical dominance after the Cold War. That trend will not be reversed in the near term: we will be a strong military power at the beginning of our next war.

We went from fighting only in or near our own country in the eighteenth and nineteenth centuries to fighting only overseas in the twentieth and twenty-first centuries. Our next war will be overseas.

Most of the wars that America has fought have been against the military forces of another country, although the enemy we oppose can certainly be insurgent or a surrogate.[2] There will be another major war and that war will be against the military forces of another nation or a group of nations.

America most often goes to war with the support of allies and we do better when that is the case. When our allied approach is more a pretext, as in Korea and Vietnam and the Iraq War, we do less well. That kind of alliance formation can't begin in the run-up to war. Real alliances, those that can sustain the sacrifices of war, come from shared values and goals.[3] NATO has been a decades-long success in part because it is a genuine political compact as well as a military alliance. We will need sustained diplomacy now if we want to have allies in our next war.

America has had to expand its military forces to fight each of its major wars. With the single exception of the Cold War—and we downsized that army when the Berlin Wall fell—we have not maintained a war-sized standing military between wars. The army we have now is a modestly sized, albeit expensive, force and is in truth a between-wars force that we mistakenly think of as our go-to-war army. When our next war comes, we will have to expand our military forces to fight it.

There will be another major war. The twentieth century saw America in four such conflicts: World War I, World War II, Korea, and Vietnam. The twenty-first century has begun with conflict and instability. Each of America's past wars was largely unanticipated. America's next war will not arrive on anyone's schedule, but it will arrive.

Our next war, then, will be against another country, overseas, and will arrive unscheduled. We will start the war as a credible military power but will have to expand our forces significantly to fight a major war. We will fight, if we are fortunate, as a part of an allied effort. All of that seems obvious once you say it, but the Pentagon and the White House often muddle fundamental issues when chasing political expediencies or budget legerdemain.

Where exactly that war will be fought is anyone's guess. A number of regional miscreants retain a conventional military capability for regional aggression. North Korea and Iran are current candidates. Failed and failing states have a habit of destabilizing military adventuring: North Korea makes this list as well, as do several African countries. Finally, there are ongoing tensions that could flare to war in short order: the Middle East, India and Pakistan, the Balkans, the Taiwan Straits. The nuclear proliferation that has already occurred can take any of those conflicts to the catastrophic in very short order.

We are not prepared to fight our next war and we are not confronting the issues now that will prepare us to fight that war when it comes. American victories require leaders of integrity and strategic insight. If the Iraq War proves nothing else, it proves that the way our presidents and generals now make decisions does not work. Whether our strategic mistakes in Iraq came from a political/military disconnect, from a lack of insight, or from politicized Washington policymaking can be debated at great length, but one fact is clear: when we needed sound policies and correct decisions, the current process consistently failed to produce them.

We are not prepared to expand our interwar army to a major war force. That failure can be squarely laid at the Pentagon's doorstep. We have a very good between-war force but have mistaken it for the force that will fight our next major war. We have given little thought and have less inclination to move to a major war force to meet the next war. Time, effort, and money spent on a long-term citizen soldier capability compete with the current Pentagon way of doing business. That is no contest: the *crisis de jour* wins every time.

We have allowed defense decisions to follow the path of least resistance, out of view and of little concern to most of our citizens. Presidents now send standing forces to war. That means our citizens and their representatives in Congress avoid the responsibility of making the decision to go to war and the responsibility of fighting those wars. Viewing war as a government program does not involve all of America when war comes. Three of our last four wars—Korea, Vietnam, and the Iraq War—have lacked the broad base of support needed for victory. If we are going to recapture the heartfelt national commitment that winning a major war requires, defending America must once again become every citizen's responsibility.

We need to know now what we are going to do when war comes. Americans are more likely to make the kind of effort and sacrifice called for if they have trust in their leaders and if the nation has been forewarned and forearmed. That is, forearmed with values and understanding, not weapons. Our leaders have not done the kinds of things necessary to earn that trust nor have they made the case—and made the hard decisions required—to get the nation ready to deter wars where we can and fight wars where we must.

The costs of mistakes in making go-to-war decisions will increase. As the circle of nuclear armed nations inexorably widens, mistakes in making go-to-war decisions become increasingly dangerous. Those that hated America in Iraq could use conventional explosives to blow up convoys in Baghdad. In the future, the weapons available to those who oppose America will be more lethal, their targets much larger, our losses much closer to home.

Matthew Ridgway offers some wisdom here. Having had to redeem a battlefield disaster in Korea, he termed our lack of preparedness there shameful. Further, he decried "political leaders—and plenty in uniform too—forlornly hoping that we can defend ourselves, save ourselves, by choosing what appears to be the easiest, cheapest path." Defending America has never been easy or cheap and it will not be in the future.

CHAPTER 16:
Our Last Victory

HISTORY HAS AN IMMEDIACY TO IT for soldiers and generals. The lessons learned in our previous victories can guide us still. America's last major victory was World War II. Although fewer and fewer of the men and women who fought that war are still with us, the lessons they learned are. World War II ended twenty years before Vietnam started, but our senior leaders in Vietnam had been captains and majors and colonels in World War II. Junior officers in Vietnam learned from them. Our Vietnam-era officers have just left the stage but they passed on their knowledge to our current senior generals and admirals. Tactics and equipment change but the fundamentals of warfighting endure. Part of all this is the way we pick leaders. George Marshall was Pershing's aide, Marshall mentored Eisenhower and Ridgway, Abrams was a Patton protégé. Today's leaders learned what they know within that lineage.

The centerpiece of the American experience in World War II occurred in an eleven-month campaign that began with the landing at Normandy and ended with the surrender of Germany. America had spent three years of nearly unrestrained effort getting ready to fight that fight. We raised an army, built factories to supply equipment, and trained soldiers and junior leaders. The outcome of those eleven months determined the outcome of the war and indeed determined the fate of much of the world.

The campaign that won World War II lacks a call to arms name that makes it easily comprehensible to people who have a life outside the military. It is most often called the European Theater of Operations, or ETO, a term that somehow doesn't do it justice. It is Normandy, the St.-Lô breakout, Patton's dash across France, the Battle of the Bulge, breaching the Siegfried Line, and crossing the Rhine. It was a huge effort. Eisenhower commanded three million men and women, thousands of ships and airplanes, tens of thousands of tanks and trucks and artillery pieces.[1] It was mostly an American force: two-thirds of the people and more than two-thirds of the equipment came from the United States.

The campaign's beginning hung by a thread. The landing at Normandy succeeded but just barely. Some key objectives that the Allied planners thought would be taken on the first day were still in German hands weeks after the landing. The Allied force ashore stalled within sight of the beach. An Allied army there had no value other than as a German target: this would be either an offensive to recapture Europe or a costly failure. Six weeks after the landing, the Allies were still slugging it out in the thick hedgerow country of Normandy. The ugly word "stalemate" was being used.[2]

The breakout at St.-Lô occurred when Eisenhower, who thought his lack of combat service in the trenches during the Great War would cripple his career, reprised a World War I tactic. To the extent that battles were won at all in World War I, they were won with the massing of artillery firepower to lay waste to an enemy defensive position so that ground forces could move forward. Eisenhower and his army group commander, Omar Bradley, did that at St.-Lô, but they did it with a new approach: Eisenhower massed his strategic bombers—1,800 B-17s—on a tactical target and leveled the German lines.[3] Bradley and Patton dashed through and didn't stop until they ran out of gas. To be more precise, mechanized forces are enabled by their logistic support. The Allied armies eventually outran their logistic capabilities by gaining ground more quickly than the logistic systems could expand. It is the kind of problem every general, in the small hours of the night, dreams of having.

When the Americans paused to build up their logistics, the still potent German Army struck back through the Ardennes forest in December 1944. That winter was the coldest in Europe in decades, fog and snow grounded the Allied Air Force, taking away one of Eisenhower's key advantages. The war devolved into an infantry battle, squads and platoons and companies digging in, firing, maneuvering, and then digging in again.

When the Germans attacked in what came to be called the Battle of the Bulge, Eisenhower seized the opportunity and attacked the flanks of the German advance as it was still unfolding. The German forces expended much of their remaining offensive power on the Ardennes gamble, although that was not at all clear at the time. Eisenhower stayed the course and kept to his broad front strategy. His army group and army commanders—Bradley and Patton and Montgomery, among others—took ground and inexorably wore down the forces to their front. Germany surrendered not when the war was lost but when their defended terrain was measured in city blocks of rubble in Berlin. Hitler knew of his own war crimes, knew his inevitable fate and was willing to expend the lives of as many Germans as it took to extend his remaining days in the bunker beneath the wrecked Chancellery.

America's home front will be a part of any future victories or there will be no victories. In World War II, America's home front went to war. There were air raid wardens enforcing blackouts in almost every city. Six hundred thousand civilian aircraft spotters were the nation's air defense surveillance system. During the war, twelve million civilians volunteered for some form of civil defense work.[4] Home and garden magazines gave advice on how to make black out curtains and basement bomb shelters more decorative.

The Depression finally ended with war spending. Tank plants were hastily built next to auto factories, aircraft plants went from making dozens of planes a year to turning out hundreds of planes a month. Women filled the jobs left or not filled by men going into uniform: in the large plants, women often approached half the work force. America hit its industrial stride and out-produced the rest of the world combined.[5]

Hollywood made movies about the war but only after talking with Roosevelt's Coordinator of Motion Pictures. The federal government, after all, controlled the materials with which films were made. Washington did not censor the movies overtly but the studios and the federal Bureau of Motion Pictures worked together to get the government's war message onto the screen.

The public expected their screen and stage heroes to be in the war and they were. Many enlisted and many of those who did not manned canteens to host men and women in uniform and far from home. Hollywood stars helped sell war bonds to support the war and toured around the world to entertain the troops. Bob Hope captured the spirit of the times when he titled his best-selling book about his many tours *I Never Left Home*. Others did their part. Publishers and authors gave up the bulk of profits and royalties on some bestsellers and perennial favorites: over a hundred million books were printed in the new paperback format and given free to the armed forces. The biggest Broadway hit of 1942, a musical comedy titled *This is the Army*, donated its considerable revenues to the Army Emergency Relief Fund.[6]

The war changed Americans' daily lives. War production diverted raw materials and much of what was eaten, consumed, or worn was in short supply. Local rationing boards were set up and ration books were issued for every man, woman, and child in America. People drove their cars as far as their rationed gas allowed and that was often not far. Rubber for car tires was scarce and even bicycles could be purchased only with a certificate of need from the government.

Schools and teachers across the country administered rationing, thus enlisting the weight of local respectability behind the program.[7] There was some evasion and there was always a black market, but most Americans complied and most compliance was voluntary. America's home front was very much a part of the war.

✶ ✶ ✶ ✶

The things that allowed the Allied victory became clear with events and time.

The Allies were fighting for a compelling cause: defending their country from imminent threat. The aggression of Germany and Japan were obvious. The nightmare years of Nazi and Japanese occupation were abhorrent. The Americans were liberators, the Germans and Japanese conquerors. Line infantry soldiers are not given to thinking in such grand terms, they have more pressing concerns to deal with. But soldiers know why they are fighting, as do their countrymen who support them. That knowledge is a source of either fundamental strength or fundamental weakness.

Allied leadership proved superior to German and Japanese leadership. Allied presidents and prime ministers, more often than not, made the correct decisions and set the right policies in place. Generals developed a sound strategy and won battles. There were admittedly missteps but in the end, Allied leaders were up to the task.

The Allies fought with citizen soldiers. Their forces could be expanded to meet the threat of a re-militarized Germany and Japan. The between-war forces of America and Britain provided senior leadership and a framework for vastly expanded armies, air forces, and navies manned by citizens turned soldiers. Hitler was convinced that his dogma-trained Wehrmacht, built on a Hitler Youth foundation, could best what he viewed as an indolent American youth and a mongrelized American culture. He was wrong. There are people in the world today who now share Hitler's former view of America.

America's values were intact. Men and women went to war because it was the right thing to do. Army values were important but the army took on the values of its citizen soldiers as much as the soldiers adopted army norms. There were no American My Lais in World War II, no organized units committing atrocities as the Germans did at Malmedy, as the Russians did routinely, and as Hitler's holocaust did on an industrial scale. Individual war crimes committed by the Allies were prosecuted and, perhaps more importantly, not accepted by other soldiers. It was a hard war, hard things were done, but the Allied Army fought within the framework of the values of the army and its soldiers.

Leader values were intact. Just days after the Normandy landing, Hitler started what was at the time called terror bombing. He began using the new V-1, the "V" standing for vengeance, a somewhat guided rocket bomb. The V-1 was so inaccurate that it had no military objective other than to terrorize civilians.[8] Allied leaders knew the even more deadly V-2 rocket would soon be operational. Winston Churchill wanted to stop the rocket attacks, which were killing thousands of Londoners: he proposed using poison gas against the launch sites on the French and Belgian coast. Eisenhower recoiled from the idea of introducing gas into the war and vetoed the proposal.[9] Eisenhower, rightly or wrongly, has detractors who find his generalship or strategic vision wanting: any general who held such a position will be pulled at by historians, and properly so. But Eisenhower was beyond question a genuinely good man and held those values through five-star rank. When his forces found the Nazi death camps, Eisenhower personally toured the worst parts of them—Patton was with him but declined the tour for fear that he would be sick—so that there could later be no question of what had happened.[10]

In World War II, all of America went to war—its economy, its people, and its science. That put large armies in the field and put the needed equipment in the hands of our troops. Advanced aircraft pushed the range and the lethality of America's combat power. A large and powerful navy carried much of the burden for the war in the Pacific. The Manhattan Project created the atomic weapons that ended the war.

The Allies went to war to defend their freedom. Germany and Japan went to war to expand their borders. Over time, the democracies' purpose proved to be more potent.

If those are the hallmarks of our last victory, it is fair—if disconcerting—to measure how the United States would do today on these same benchmarks. Disconcerting because we are not doing well.

We go to war now for causes of only passing importance. More than two centuries of American experience of Congressional declarations of war and citizens then taking up arms to fight those wars has been turned on its head. Presidents now decide on their own initiative to take the nation to war and then send standing military forces off to fight those wars. That has allowed the causes for war to become less compelling. We have let politicians cry wolf too often. Vietnam was fought for a domino theory that proved illusory. The Iraq War was fought to prevent the use of weapons of mass destruction that did not exist. There is now a global threat of terrorism, but that threat is not a war. When a real war comes, our leaders will have diluted the impact of the very idea of war and will have squandered the moral authority that war leaders must have.

Our defense decision making is broken. The presidency and the Pentagon have become politicized and bureaucratized. Presidents have always looked to reelection, but it is certain that George Washington and Abraham Lincoln and Theodore Roosevelt would risk reelection for a principle. It is likely that Franklin Roosevelt, Truman, and Eisenhower would have as well. It is clear that presidents since then have not.

Civilian leaders in the Pentagon in World War II were men of prominence and success who made significant sacrifices to serve the nation. There were not many of them and, if they were a somewhat exclusive white man's club, they were a club that valued gentlemanly conduct: politics were an only tolerated part of their world. The number of civilian defense officials after World War II proliferated. Politics became how they got the job in the first place, how they kept the job, and how they advanced. Often any prominence or financial success they had came as a result of their Pentagon tenure. There were exceptions at both ends of this description but we have by and large reversed a process that worked and we now have a process that does not work.

We have gone to war too often since World War II. The last general to dissuade a president from going to war was Matthew Ridgway in 1954. We needed that kind of forceful senior military counsel going into Vietnam and Iraq but such counsel did not make it into final policymaking for either conflict. Presidents and secretaries of defense determine the level and weight of the military counsel they receive and they have done that poorly. We need to revert to the previous Roosevelt/Marshall ground rules. Presidents and senior generals and admirals need to develop the direct trust and confidence between each other that war decisions demand.

Blithely assuming that Americans can win a major war in our future because previous generations of Americans have done so in the past is a dangerous illusion. In the end, it should be our purpose now that our last major victory, World War II, does not become our last victory.

CHAPTER 17:
Solutions

THERE ARE SOLUTIONS to the challenges we face if we will be bold in grasping them.

Return to citizen soldier armies

If it is citizens who become the soldiers who fight our wars, we are more likely to go to war only for compelling causes. We must demand of Congress that they meet their clear constitutional duty to declare wars—or not—on our behalf. Elective or preemptive wars where presidents send standing forces off to war on their own authority make going to war too easy by far. That flawed approach has taken us to stalemate in Korea, defeat in Vietnam, and misadventure in Iraq. It is time to stop.

We now spend almost all our effort and resources to achieve short-term tactical dominance for our standing military and almost none of our effort and resources in preparing to expand our forces in time of war. We assume that our wars will be fought with the army we have, which is patently wrong. Our past victories came not from the armies we had when the war started but from the armies we could build. In the long run, whether we are five times technologically better than our nearest current adversary or ten times technologically better than our nearest current adversary is less important than maintaining the bonds between our citizens and our soldiers.

The first of our victories—the American Revolution—gave us a country and it was fought by necessity with citizen soldiers. That was the only army the colonists had. George Washington was the general in the field commanding that army and he was central to its victory. When he called his force a patriot army, it was not an idle compliment: he knew that citizen soldiers fighting for their freedom would beat a mercenary army every time. There can be no American Hessians, nor should there be. The drafters of our Constitution were veterans of the Revolution: almost all served in either the Continental Congress or in the army.[1] Washington presided over the Constitutional Convention and his patriot army views passed into the very core of the Constitution. Defense of the new nation was based on the army that had won their war: America would fight its wars with citizen soldier armies.

We ought to heed the echo from the French commander at Dien Bien Phu in Vietnam. In trying to explain his series of defeats, Brig. Gen. Christian de Castries cited the "inevitable" advantage in morale of troops fighting for freedom in their own country over the morale of foreign troops fighting under contract.[2] George Washington would have understood immediately: de Castries was describing Washington's patriot army. That is the army we should have now.

Today, defense of the nation touches few Americans directly, which diminishes our strength. An American war must be all of America's war. We can do that by re-tethering the American military to the American people. We can do that with broad-based national service that helps fill our future ranks with citizen soldiers in time of need. That will bring the full weight of America's power to bear when war comes.

Hold our leaders to a higher standard

We must have presidents who place the good of the nation ahead of their reelection prospects. We must have senior military officers who will risk their careers pressing unwelcome views on civilian leaders. Presidents get to be president because citizens vote them into office: we get the leaders we demand and we are not demanding enough.

Restore senior officers to final defense decision making

Generals and admirals must give presidents direct and forceful counsel on go-to-war decisions. Civilians set the manner and tone of such counsel and they have set it badly. Our ability today to bring strategic vision to bear is hampered by distancing our senior military officers from final policymaking and by winnowing out the independent counsel that senior officers should bring to the process. The successful Roosevelt-Marshall model is long past. The potential for even a Ridgway-type disruption, for an individual officer to force hard choices on a president, has gone a glimmering. Our ability to marshal strategic insight is not a given. We can do that successfully, as we did in Desert Storm, and we can do that unsuccessfully, as we did in the Iraq War. Presidents and generals need to look each other in the eye and understand what the other is saying.

We must recapture the directness of the Roosevelt-Marshall model for defense decision making. The temple keepers of the current Washington bureaucracy would have us believe that issues today are too complex to do that. Not so. The layers of committees and commissions that have replaced individuals making decisions hinder more than they help. Much of our current bureaucracy is in place to avoid accountability for the consequences of making difficult decisions.

Develop a coherent defense strategy

In the American military, strategy drives requirements. We are chasing events for want of a strategy. That makes wars both more likely to occur and harder to win. A coherent strategy makes wars less likely and more winnable. The strategy we need now is to build the capability to fight a major war, use our standing forces between wars to contain crises and small wars, and deal with emerging threats such as terrorism. That strategy may or may not require a larger army but it will require a different army. We must plan now to expand to a citizen soldier army when the next war finds us.

Honor our values

Values define our army. They allow our officers and soldiers to meet the ethical rigors of combat. They allow senior officers to advise presidents and secretaries of defense well and forthrightly. They allow our military to be among the guarantors of our freedom. Strong values come from honor, tradition, leadership, and mentoring. They are a tie to our past and a lifeline for our future.

Go to war only to defend America's freedom

Our strength is in our ideals, our commitment to freedom, and our citizens' willingness to defend that freedom. If America is attacked by military forces, our response should be massive and remorseless. If we are threatened by something other than a military attack, our soft power assets—an updated version of the Marshall Plan—are a better early response. Freedom has been the linchpin of America's victories. World War II was about defending America's freedom. Korea and Vietnam were about opposing Communism. Iraq was about opposing something, not making the world "safe for," but making the world "safe from." Through misuse, we have today misplaced the wisdom of going to war only to defend America's freedom.

Defending freedom can guide America's role as a global power in the future. If America's freedom is at risk, war is justified. If America's freedom is not at risk, something may be called for, but not taking America to war.

It would be the worst of misjudgments to assume that America will not be called upon to fight wars in our future and the worst of mistakes to be unprepared to fight those wars when they come. Future victories require hard choices and unremitting effort now.

We will have to rebuild our army after Iraq. That means we have to look to our values, our people, our equipment, and our leadership. We rebuilt our army successfully after Vietnam and we can again. If we are clever, rebuilding becomes an opportunity.

The process after Vietnam was painful and time consuming. Senior leaders set a course to fix the army's values: a baseline integrity, doing the right thing for the right reasons. Do what is best for the mission, for the troops, and only then—and this is a distant third— what is best for yourself. Leaders of integrity only want to be around other leaders of integrity, good soldiers only want to be around other good soldiers. The army's rebuilding after Iraq will be easier than after Vietnam. The challenges we face now are less deep-seated than the challenges we faced then.

The easy part of rebuilding is the equipment. After Desert Storm, our army could not have deployed around the corner, much less around the world, for eighteen months because our equipment was broken and out of place. Mounds and fields of equipment were stored at docks in the Middle East, then brought to the United States and reconditioned and then sent to our units. And that was from a one-hundred-hour war. Iraq has been a years-long war with enormous usage and substantial combat damage. Getting our equipment returned and fixed or replaced will take years.

Leadership is the critical piece in rebuilding our force after Iraq. The right leadership will let us fix the other problems. We have good junior leaders—sergeants and lieutenants and captains—in our army. The challenge will be to keep them in the army. We have over-used them and their families in Iraq. They will stay if we let them be soldiers, if we give them an environment of sound values and good senior leaders. We have the tools at hand to do that but will need support from civilian policymakers in Washington. The army needs a breather, no more good ideas or flawed preemptive wars for a while. Left moderately alone, the army will fix itself.

The real challenge is the next generation of senior leaders, generals and admirals who have the intellectual heft to makes sense of difficult policy issues and a penchant for pressing hard choices on presidents and secretaries of defense. Those officers are there. But it is senior civilian leaders who must let them fulfill their obligations as warriors and counselors. Such counsel is properly offered only in private, but there is a very public way of knowing how well that process is working. A White House or an Office of the Secretary of Defense that keeps a chokehold on information and defaults to a political spin approach in times of crisis will be unlikely to find the tolerance for senior officer dissent. And dissent should be an everyday part of the process.

It is politically incorrect in the Pentagon to deviate from the joint mantra, but the fact is that all military services are not created equal. The army, navy, air force, and marines all bring different things to the warfight, get used up at different rates, and will have different needs coming out of Iraq. The air force will not need to be rebuilt after Iraq, they just need new airplanes. The navy will not have to be rebuilt after Iraq, they just need new ships. If the rest of the Pentagon doesn't try overly much to help, the marine corps will regenerate after Iraq on its own. The need to rebuild is in the army, which bore the brunt of the war in Iraq and which will continue to carry the bulk of our interwar engagement workload in the future.

We will have to retrain our army for conventional war. That means taking a part of the force and fencing it off from other missions. That will not be a display army. A trained and ready force is a deterrent and can fill the breach in a no-notice war while the rest of our forces expand and deploy. That retraining will take several years once begun.

We have to make our army expandable into a larger army, potentially a much larger army. George Marshall ramped up our army in World War II and we can do that in the future if we recognize the need now and put in place the pathways now that will take us forward. That will take leadership on a George Marshall scale, which is asking a lot. But our current leaders are up to the task.

We need to let our full-time interwar force perform the full-time interwar missions. That is containing small wars and crises to prevent major wars. That is developing tactics, doctrine, and maintaining high soldier standards. A portion of our standing force should be the fenced core around which we expand to a major warfight force. Half of the units in our war plans now are from the Guard and reserve. If we can truly put the long-standing and debilitating active/reserve component turf battle behind us, we can add major combat units from the Guard to our war plans. They will have the six months of lift-driven delay in deploying that will let them complete their war training. That will free up active-duty forces for interwar engagements that avoid wars in the first place. If we assume that everyone who wears a nametape that says U.S. Army on it is in the U.S. Army—and that includes active, Guard, and reserve soldiers—we can capture the strengths of all parts of our army and match those strengths to the missions we face.

One of the unforeseen casualties of our Pentagon missioning by bureaucracy has been the core value that defense of the country is every citizen's obligation. Services defending their turf, presidents their reelection, and generals their careers are unlikely to tell America's citizens that they and their families will have to bear the sacrifices of going to war. But just as presidents have the final say over generals, citizens have the final say over presidents. If this issue is to be fixed, it will be fixed by our citizens' understanding and expectations, not by our politicians.

America's past is America's promise. Our military power has been best used in the pursuit of freedom: first to win a nation, then to preserve that nation, then to defend it. Since World War II, the United States has turned its power and position to seek a more peaceful and stable world, to assist other nations in their move toward freedom.

The promise of America is the promise of the idea that people ought to be free. The ideas of Jefferson's era still ring true. Reason will best order our affairs and individual freedom extends the reach of that reason. Free citizens will advance themselves and their communities and their nation. The first duty of a government is to protect that freedom.

Other forms of governments have had other purposes: the privilege of rulers, the dictates of a given religion, the pursuit of empire. America, in the main, has not sought to inflict its purpose on other nations. We have sought to protect our own freedom and the freedom of others. In the post–Cold War world, American sponsorship of freedom is an opportunity for those who would seek it, not a requirement mandated from the United States.

If America is to fulfill its promise of freedom, to itself and to the rest of the world, the American military will play a role. The United States must have a strategy that makes sense. That means protecting our warfighting ability, focusing our interwar engagement missions and dealing with emerging threats such as terrorism. The issues there are knowable, the tasks doable.

America must have forces that are capable of executing that strategy. The strength of those forces comes from re-tethering them to the American people, from being guided by our shared values, and from growing bold leaders of sense and integrity. Good leaders make soldiers better than they think they can be. If an American commander has high expectations of his soldiers, leads them by example, leads from the front, and does the right thing for the right reason, soldiers will perform extraordinary feats. That is why, on some days in some places, the description that uncommon valor was commonplace becomes quite literally true. It happened at Normandy and at the Ia Drang. It can happen again.

America and its military share high expectations of each other. Soldiers go to war for America because America is worth going to war for. And a nation of high purpose, which can field so good a force, will try to live up to the expectations of its soldiers.

There is a rhythm to this business of soldiering. Waking up in a barracks involves someone shouting. Physical training as the sun comes up, then draw weapons and equipment and move out to a training area. Squads and platoons and companies. The day will be long and outdoors and hard, learning and practicing the skills of war.

Night is back to the barracks, clean equipment and weapons then yourself. At eleven, they play taps. Not because someone has died but because it is the end of a duty day. The next day starts early. Weeks and months pass, seasons change, years fly by. War changes the events of the day but not the rhythm. It is still weapons and other soldiers, doing the things you trained so hard to do, still arduous work, far from home and family. Fear is a background feeling. The occasional terror of combat is so intense that it passes. If you have done this, you understand one of Creighton Abrams' favorite sayings: Soldiering is an affair of the heart.[3]

There is a rhythm to defending America. It started with an idea, that all people are free to seek their own destiny. It took an American Revolution, the rhythm of soldiering, to make that happen. When America was torn into two warring halves, it was the soldiering that brought it back together. The politicians failed at the task, although Lincoln's wisdom was profound. America was rejoined by force of arms. When Lee and Grant met at Appomattox, the war had scarred America deeply. But Lee and Grant and their soldiers knew that the war was past and their task was to now become citizens again. The politicians may not have known that but the soldiers did.

As America grew to a position of world power, that rhythm of soldiering grew to fill the space of those larger concerns: Theodore Roosevelt's canal and the Great White Fleet, an American Expeditionary Force in World War I and in Normandy in World War II, garrisoning Europe for four decades in the Cold War. Men and women fought in foreign lands with the courage and commitment those before them had learned on American soil. The places were different but the purpose was the same.

The world has changed, the mechanics of war have changed, but the deep currents, the rhythm of defending America, have not changed. It is still Americans going into harm's way to serve a cause they think is important, a cause worth risking their lives for. We can have as good a military as we have ever had. The young men and women in our ranks, in their understated way, are magnificent. Our officers can be as good as any leaders in our history, if we let them. The challenge is to hear the rhythm, to know the deep currents. Go to war for compelling causes, take all of America to war. Trust our citizens to be soldiers. Believe in our values. Defend freedom. That rhythm will renew America's military might and assure America's victories in the future.

On the day he was to die, Lincoln related to his cabinet a recurring dream he often had before momentous events. In that dream, Lincoln was on a boat, sailing across dark waters toward a distant, indefinite shore. The most destructive war in America's history was just days from being over. No one, certainly not Lincoln, knew what lay ahead, what shape that shore would take.

America is still moving toward that distant shore. Much of the rest of the world travels with us now. Safe havens lie ahead if we have the skill and courage to make the journey.

Notes

PREFACE

1. The information age can be monumentally disconcerting. A picture of my Ranger team getting awards for this mission is on the Web at http://www.lrrprangers.com/f-PicIndex.htm, Vietnam Photos 31, Olivas Team.

INTRODUCTION

1. "Spending: CRS Report for Congress, Comparisons of U.S. and Foreign Military Spending: Data from Selected Public Sources," (January 28, 2004): 5. In 1939, the army had fewer than 200,000 troops and the United States had a population of 130 million. Today, we have an active duty army of 512,000 and a population of 300 million.

CHAPTER 1

1. Stephen E. Ambrose, *D-Day: June 6, 1944, The Climatic Battle of World War II* (New York: Simon & Schuster, 1994), 320–360.
2. Geoffrey Perret, *There's a War to Be Won: The United States Army in World War II* (New York: Ivy Books, 1991), 320.
3. Michael D. Doubler, *I Am the Guard: A History of the Army National Guard, 1636-2000* (Department of the Army Phamplet No. 130-1, 2001), 166.
4. Max Hastings, *Overlord: D-Day and the Battle for Normandy* (New York: Simon & Schuster, 1984), 86–102.
5. David Halberstam, *War in a Time of Peace: Bush, Clinton, and the Generals* (New York: Scribner, 2001), 122.

6. Author tour of Sarajevo in 2007 with the commander of Bosnian forces during the siege, LTG Jovan Divjak.

7. General Wesley K. Clark, USA (Ret.), "Waging Modern War: Bosnia, Kosovo, and the Future of Conflict" (New York: Public Affairs, 2001): 49; *The New York Times* (27 May 1995): 1, 1.

8. http://www.af.mil/factsheets/factsheet.asp?fsID=83.

9. *Army Times* (25 February 2008): 1.

10. I got this bit of wisdom, expressed with his usual clarity, from my friend and mentor, the late General Wayne A. Downing, USA.

11. "Congressional Research Service Report for Congress: Potential Navy Force Structure and Shipbuilding Plans: Background and Issues for Congress" (Updated 30 March 2005): 12.

Chapter 2

1. Douglas Kinnard, *The Secretary of Defense* (Lexington, KT: UP of Kentucky, 1980), 17.

2. Thomas E. Ricks, *Fiasco: The America Military Adventure in Iraq* (New York: Penguin Press, 2006), 76, 122.

3. Doubler, *I Am the Guard*, 138.

4. Halberstam, *War in a Time of Peace*, 436.

5. Forrest C. Pogue, *George C. Marshall: Education of a General* (New York: Viking Press, 1963), 322–323; Thomas Parrish, *Roosevelt and Marshall: Partners in Politics and War* (New York: William Morrow and Co., Inc., 1989), 16–18.

6. Ibid., 297.

7. H. R. McMaster, *Dereliction of Duty: Lyndon Johnson, Robert McNamara, the Joint Chiefs of Staff, and the Lies that Led to Vietnam* (New York: Harper Collins, 1997), 28; Arthur M. Schlesinger, Jr., *A Thousand Days* (Boston: Houghton Mifflin Co., 1965), 296–297; Maxwell D. Taylor, recorded interviews by Elsbeth Rostow, 12 April 1964, 7 and 21 June 1964, 28, John F. Kennedy Oral History Program, John F. Kennedy Library, Boston, MA; Deputy Secretary of Defense Roswell L. Gilpatrick, recorded interview with Dennis J. O'Brien, 5 May 1970, 14, John F. Kennedy Oral History Program, John F. Kennedy Library, Boston, MA.

8. McMaster, *Dereliction of Duty*, 62.

9. Lewis Sorley, *Honorable Warrior: General Harold K. Johnson and the Ethics of Command* (Lawrence, KS: UP of Kansas, 1998), 222–223. The nervous major went on to a distinguished career and wrote a book: Lt. Gen. Charles G. Cooper (Ret.), *Cheers and Tears: A Marine's Story of Combat in Peace and War* (Reno, NV: Wesley Press, 2002), 1–5.

10. McMaster, *Dereliction of Duty*, 163.

11. The Pentagon Papers, Volume II, 160. Usually an invaluable aid to historians on Vietnam policymaking, the Pentagon Papers are suspect in their treatment of Kennedy's decision to withdraw from Vietnam. By the time the Pentagon Papers study was conducted, the war was going very badly. No staffer could expect to keep his job by telling Johnson that Kennedy had it right on Vietnam if, in fact, Kennedy had it right on Vietnam.

12. Michael R. Gordon and Lt. Gen. Bernard E. Trainor, USMC (Ret.), *Cobra II: The Inside Story of the Invasion and Occupation of Iraq* (New York: Pantheon Books, 2006), 32.

13. The Pentagon is moving from threat-based war plans—what we might have to do—to a capabilities-based process: what we can do. Either way, if we tell ourselves the truth, it is a big workload.

CHAPTER 3

1. Richard L. Russell, "CIA's Strategic Intelligence in Iraq," *Political Science Quarterly* 117 (2002): 195.

2. Brigadier General Robert H. Scales, Jr., *Certain Victory: United States Army in the Gulf War* (Washington, D.C.: Office of the Chief of Staff, United States Army, 1993), 45.

3. Department of the Navy, Naval Historical Center, "The Gathering Storm: The Build-up of U.S. Forces," 1, http://www.history.navy.mil/wars/dstorm/ds2.htm.

4. Scales, *Certain Victory*, 50.

5. General H. Norman Schwarzkopf, *It Doesn't Take a Hero* (New York: Linda Grey Bantam Books, 1992), 312.

6. Ibid., 412.

7. Gunnery Sergeant John D. Cornwell, USMCR.

8. Command chronology dated 17 March 1991, reference number MCO 5750.1F; interview with Alpha Company commander, Captain (later Colonel) Michael J. Hussey and input from Gunnery Sergeant Cornwell.

9. Schwarzkopf, *It Doesn't Take a Hero*, 325.

10. Gordon and Trainor, *Cobra II*, 28.

11. Ricks, *Fiasco*, 69.

12. Ibid., 97.

13. "Iraqi Women Prepare for Democratic Election," http://www.whitehouse.gov/infocus/elections/facts.html#.

14. Ricks, *Fiasco*, 272.

15. *Jane's World Armies*, Jane's Information Group Limited, Sentinel House, Surrey CR5 2TH, UK, 832.

CHAPTER 4

1. Forrest C. Pogue, *George C. Marshall: Ordeal and Hope* (New York: Viking Press, 1965), 123–124.

2. "Twenty-seven Articles," *Arab Bulletin* (20 August 1917), reprinted in T.E. Lawrence, *Secret Dispatches [sic] from Arabia*, A. W. Lawrence, ed. (London: Golden Cockerel Press, 1939), 126–133. http://telawrence.net/telawrencenet/works/.

3. John F. Kennedy, interview with Walter Cronkite, *CBS News*, 2 September 1963.

4. *United States Government Manual*, 1945, First Edition (Washington, DC: GPO, 1945), 248; *United States Government Organization Manual*, 1965–1966 (Washington, DC: GPO, 1965), 129–131, 144–146.

CHAPTER 5

1. Perret, *There's a War to Be Won*, 178.

2. Julian Jackson, *The Fall of France, The Nazi Invasion of 1940* (Oxford, England: Oxford UP, 2003), 27.

3. General Barry McCaffrey, USA (Ret.), admittedly a general of considerable enthusiasm.

CHAPTER 6

1. The army is shifting operational emphasis to the brigade level within the existing divisions and corps, clearly a step in the right direction.

2. Army chiefs of staff have a practice of repetition, each has a signature briefing that tries to capture the main thrust of their four-year tour as

chief. General Rick Shenseki's was on transformation, and he is the source of the armored volume analysis.

3. A.J. Bacevich, *The Pentomic Era: The U.S. Army Between Korea and Vietnam* (Washington, D.C: National Defense University, 1986), 95–96.

4. Ambrose, *Citizen Soldiers*, 71–72.

5. Perret, *There's a War to Be Won*, 334.

CHAPTER 7

1. War stories are always suspect, even this general officer war story told to the author.

2. Perry H. Merrill, *Roosevelt's Forest Army: A History of the Civilian Conservation Corps* (Montpelier, VT: Perry H. Merrill, 1981) 55–106.

3. Ibid., vii.

4. Williamson Murray and Allan R. Millett, *A War to be Won: Fighting the Second World War* (Cambridge, MA: Belknap Press of Harvard UP, 2000), 547.

5. Address by LTG Benjamin C. Freakley, Commander of U.S. Army Accessions Command, Ft. Knox, Kentucky, 13 July 2007.

6. Allan R. Millett and Peter Maslowski, *For the Common Defense: A Military History of the United States of America* (New York Free Press, A Division of Macmillan, Inc., 1984), 323.

7. Marc Wortman, *The Millionaires' Unit: The Aristocratic Flyboys Who Fought the Great War and Invented American Air Power* (New York: Public Affairs, 2006), 77, 92.

8. David McCullough, *Truman* (New York: Simon & Schuster, 1992), 255.

9. Carlo D'Este, *Patton: A Genius for War* (New York: Harper Collins, 1995), 383–384.

10. Phillip Ardery, *Bomber Pilot: A Memoir of World War II* (Lexington, KY: UP of Kentucky, 1978), 199.

11. Richard Lingeman, *Don't You Know There's a War On? The American Home Front, 1941–1945* (New York: Thunder's Mouth Press, 1970), 311.

12. Ambrose, *D-Day*, 493.

CHAPTER 8

1. Doubler, *I Am the Guard*, 31.

2. Geoffrey Perret, *A Country Made by War: From the Revolution to Vietnam—The Story of America's Rise to Power* (New York: Random House, 1989), 77.

3. Ibid., 171.

4. Millett and Maslowski, *For the Common Defense*, 154.

5. William Manchester, *The Last Lion: Winston Spencer Churchill, Visions of Glory, 1874-1932* (Boston: Little, Brown and Co., 1983), 574–583. Predictably, Churchill argued for a brigade command.

6. Thích Quang Duc was the first of these monks to burn himself to death. The car that drove him from Hue to Saigon is today preserved as a kind of relic at a Buddhist temple in Hue. That car is in the famous Pulitzer Prize–winning photograph that played such a significant role in highlighting the problems of the Diem régime.

7. Robert S. McNamara, *In Retrospect: The Tragedy and Lessons of Vietnam* (New York: Times Books, 1995), 216.

8. *Pentagon Papers*, 4:548.

9. Gareth Porter, ed., *Vietnam Documentation: The Definitive Documentation of Human Decisions* (Stanfordville, NY: Earl M. Coleman Enterprises, Inc., 1979), 2: 497–500.

10. David Herbert Donald, *Lincoln* (New York: A Touchstone Book published by Simon & Schuster, 1996), 448.

11. Major Michael W. Davidson, USAR, "Senior Officers and Vietnam Policymaking," *Parameters: The Journal of the Army War College* (Spring 1986): 91.

12. 50 U.S. Code, Section 1541 to 1544, passed over President Nixon's veto.

13. Stephen E. Ambrose, *Eisenhower: Soldier, General of the Army, President-Elect 1890-1952* (New York: Simon & Schuster, 1983), 127, 180.

CHAPTER 9

1. Pogue, *Ordeal and Hope*, 293–298.

2. Ambrose, *Eisenhower*, 71–72.

3. Perret, *There's a War to Be Won*, 66.

4. The Joint Requirements Oversight Council. General David Jones, USAF (Ret.).

6. Col. Charles A. Beckwith, USA (Ret.), *Delta Force* (San Diego, CA: Harcourt, 1983), 5–7, 218–219.

7. Robert Dallek, *An Unfinished Life: John F. Kennedy 1917–1963* (Boston, MA: Little, Brown and Co., 2003), 289–290.

8. Ibid., 304–5, 351.

9. Assistant National Security Adviser Walt W. Rostow, Memorandum to McGeorge Bundy, 30 January 1961, The Papers of President Kennedy, National Security Files: Vietnam, Box 193, John F. Kennedy Library, Boston, MA. This memo will quicken a researcher's heart: it begins with a request for the addressee to destroy the memo after reading.

10. Dallek, *Unfinished Life*, 368.

11. Douglas Kinnard, *The Certain Trumpet: Maxwell Taylor & The American Experience in Vietnam* (Washington: Brassey's (U.S.) Inc., 1991), 56–58.

12. People trying to find ways to criticize the handling of the Iraq War will see the appointment of a general officer as the "War Czar," the Deputy National Security Adviser, as a repetition of the Taylor misstep. That is probably not a fair comparison.

13. David Halberstam, *The Best and the Brightest* (New York: Random House, 1972), 191.

14. *The Pentagon Papers, The Defense Department History of United States Decisionmaking on Vietnam*, The Senator Gravel Edition (Boston, MA: Beacon Press, 1971), 2: 237–239.

15. Diem and his brother were buried in adjoining graves marked only with the words "two brothers." After the communist takeover of South Vietnam in 1975, the bodies were exhumed and their final disposition is unclear. Author visits to Vietnam.

16. Gareth Porter, ed., *Vietnam: A History in Documents* (New York: Times Mirror, 1981), 295.

17. McNamara deserves credit for his candor. Two decades after Vietnam, he published a book that recounts his errors with the permanence of the printed word. Robert S. McNamara, *In Retrospect: The Tragedy and Lessons of Vietnam* (New York: Times Books, 1995).

18. For those drawn to the intricacies of the Pentagon process, CJCS delivers his evaluation of the services' budget proposals in the Chairman's Program Assessment and his evaluation of the overall strategy in the

Chairman's Program Review. Both are annual documents delivered by CJCS to SECDEF without other distribution.

19. Barbara W. Tuchman, *Stilwell and the American Experience in China 1911–45* (New York: MacMillan, 1970), 50.

20. The German M-262 jet fighter was a more capable airplane but was introduced too late to have an impact on the course of the war.

21. This observation and phrasing are not mine, it is a widely used description of unclear origin. For example: Perret, *A Country Made by War*, 64.

22. Ron Chernow, *Alexander Hamilton* (New York: Penguin Books, 2004), 182.

23. H.W. Brands, *The First American: The Life and Times of Benjamin Franklin* (New York: Random House, 2000), 667–668; Bruce Chadwick, *George Washington's War: The Forging of a Revolutionary Leader and the American Presidency* (Napierville, Illinois: Sourcebooks, 2005), 443–6.

24. Jay Winik, *April 1865: The Month That Saved America* (New York: HarperCollins, 2001), 146.

25. Ibid., 147–166.

26. Ulysses S. Grant, Personal Memoirs, The Modern Library, New York, 1999, 581.

27. Halberstam, *Best and Brightest*, 593–594.

28. Briefing by Secretary of Defense Richard Cheney, Adjutants General Association of the United States, Washington, DC, Mid-winter Conference, 1990.

29. The awkwardly named *Quadrennial Defense Review*.

30. FY 2009 DOD budget: http://www.defenselink.mil/comptroller/fy2009_mil.pdf.

31. OSD-PA message to CINCs, 10 February 2003.

Chapter 10

1. Charles L. Mee, Jr., *The Marshall Plan, The Launching of the Pax Americana* (New York: Simon & Schuster, 1984), 17–18, 97.

2. Ibid., 70; Murray and Millett, *War To Be Won*, 561.

3. Manchester, *The Last Lion*, 7.

4. McCullough, *Truman*, 487.

5. *The Washington Post*, 10 April 1963, p. A1.

6. Winston S. Churchill, address, Westminster College, Fulton, Missouri, 5 March 1946.

7. McCullough, *Truman*, 489.

8. Forrest C. Pogue, *George C. Marshall: Statesman* (New York: Viking, 1987), 213–214, 525–528.

9. Mee, *Marshall Plan*, 246–258.

10. McCullough, *Truman*, 564–565. http://measuringworth.com/ calculators/uscompare/. This useful site for comparing the present value of previous year sums was referenced in David Nasaw, *Andrew Carnegie* (New York: Penguin Press, 2006), 85.

11. Merrill Peterson, *The Jeffersonian Image in the American Mind* (New York: Oxford UP, 1960), 234; cited in Gordon S. Wood, *Revolutionary Characters, What Made the Founders Different* (New York: Penguin Press, 2006), 94.

12. Joseph J. Ellis, *American Sphinx: The Character of Thomas Jefferson* (New York: Alfred A. Knopf, 1997), 107.

13. Catherine Drinker Bowen, *Miracle at Philadelphia: The Story of the Constitutional Convention, May to September 1787* (Boston, MA: Little, Brown and Co., 1966), 135.

14. Christopher Crittenden, *The American Historical Review*, Vol. 54, No. 1 (Oct. 1948): 151.

15. Ralph Peters address at The Army War College 11 Annual Strategy Conference, 2000; Samuel Huntington, *The Clash of Civilizations and the Remaking of World Order* (New York: Simon & Schuster, 1996), 210 and generally.

16. Thomas L. Friedman, *The World is Flat* (New York: Farrar, Straus and Giroux, 2005), 249 and generally.

17. Huntington, *Clash of Civilizations*, 207–238.

18. Robert Kagan, *Of Paradise and Power* (New York: Alfred A. Knopf, 2003), 3–11.

19. General Wesley K. Clark, USA (Ret.), who was not amused.

20. One of several "Tokyo Roses," Iva Toquri D'Aquino was later pardoned by President Gerald Ford when two of her accusers said D'Aquino had been coerced.

21. Halberstam, *War in a Time of Peace*, 248–254.

22. Williamson Murray, "The United States Should Begin Work on a New Bomber Now," *Policy Analysis* 368 (2000): 6.

23. http://www.acepilots.com/planes/main.html.

24. www.atimes.com/atimes/cjina/JA08Ad01.html.

25. "Congressional Research Service Report for Congress: China Naval Modernization: Implications for U.S. Navy Capabilities-Background and Issues for Congress." 18 November 2005: 1, 6–9.

Chapter 11

1. Department of the Navy, Naval Historical Center Online Library: People, Japan. Yamamoto's knowledge was not casual: like most attachés then and now, broad-based intelligence gathering was a part of his duties.

2. Murray and Millett, *A War to Be Won*, 150.

3. Perret, *A Country Made by War*, 362.

4. Murray and Millett, *A War to Be Won*, 535.

5. Ibid., 536.

6. Manchester, *The Last Lion*, 54.

7. Jackson, *Fall of France*, 23–25.

8. Thomas C. Hone, Norman Friedman, and Mark D. Mandeles, *American and British Aircraft Carrier Development, 1919–1941* (Annapolis, MD: Naval Institute Press, 1999), 51–59.

9. Ibid., 25–50.

10. Mee, *Marshall Plan*, 21.

11. David Frum and Richard Perle, *An End to Evil: How to Win the War on Terror* (New York: Random House, 2003), 203.

12. Center for Strategic and Budgetary Assessments: http://www.csbaonline.org/2006-1/2.DefenseBudget/Topline.shtml.

13. http://www.whitehouse.gov/omb/budget/fy2007/pdf/hist.pdf.

14. General Peter Schoomacher, USA, Army Chief of Staff, Defense Forum Foundation address to the Congressional Defense and Foreign Policy Forum, "U.S. Army's Role and Needs for Fighting the War on Terror," 14 July 2006.

15. FY 2009 DOD budget: http://www.defenselink.mil/comptroller/fy2009_mil.pdf.

16. Bomber: Williamson Murray, "The United States Should Begin Work on a New Bomber Now," *Policy Analysis* 368 (2000): 4. Carrier: "CRS Report for Congress: Defense Department Procurement: Full Funding Policy-Background, Issues and Options for Congress" (Updated June 28, 2005): 7. Destroyer: Raytheon, Products & Services, DD(X) program http://www.raytheon.com/products/ddx/.

17. Center for Strategic and Budgetary Assessments: http://www.csbaonline.org/2006-1/2.DefenseBudget/Topline.shtml.

18. Manchester, *The Last Lion*, 123–125.

19. Ibid., 424.

CHAPTER 12

1. Forrest C. Pogue, *George C. Marshall: Organizer of Victory* (New York: Viking Press, 1973) 584.

2. Pogue, *Ordeal and Hope*, 1, 6.

3. Defensive strategically. The campaign in the Pacific was a series of limited operational offenses.

4. Pogue, *Ordeal and Hope*, 22. The most obvious advantage to an earlier end of the war against Japan would have been the availability of additional landing craft, a bottleneck in the European Theater. Other than as a negotiating ploy used against our British allies, the plan remained throughout the war to defeat Germany first, then Japan.

5. Ibid., 314–317.

6. Millett and Maslowski, *For the Common Defense*, 357.

7. Pogue, *Ordeal and Hope*, 154.

8. Atomic bomb: Perret, *There's a War to Be Won*, 529.

9. Doubler, *I Am the Guard*, 195–201.

10. Ambrose, *To America*, 94.

11. Pogue, *Education of a General*, re: the CCC: 274–277; re: the Illinois National Guard: 281–282.

12. Pogue, *Organizer of Victory*, xi.

13. Grant, *Memoirs*, 189.

14. Don M. Snyder, et al. "Army Professionalism, the Military Ethic and Officership in the 21 Century." Strategic Studies Institute, U.S. Army War College, December 1999.

15. D'este, *Patton*, 131.

16. Dwight D. Eisenhower, *At Ease: Stories I Tell to Friends* (Garden City, NY: Doubleday & Co., Inc, 1967), 155–166.

17. Lowell Thomas and Edward Jablonski, *Doolittle: A Biography* (Garden City, NY: Doubleday & Company, 1976), 121–127.

18. There is some question as to whether Ridgway was eased out or left by his own choice. Suffice to say that most chiefs serve two two-year terms. Ridgway served one.

19. Sorley, *Honorable Warrior*, 304.

20. Admiral William J. Fallon, USN, Central Command. *Washington Post*, (12 March 2008): 1, 1.

21. Chadwick, *George Washington's War*, 303.

22. Horace Porter, *Campaigning With Grant* (New York: The Century Co., 1897), 59.

23. William Manchester, *American Caesar: Douglas MacArthur 1880–1964* (Boston, MA: Little, Brown and Co., 1978), 101–102.

24. Geoffrey Perret, *Eisenhower* (New York: Random House, 1999), 295.

25. James M. Gavin, *On to Berlin: Battles of An Airborne Commander 1943–1946* (New York: Viking Press, 1978), 106–109.

26. Callum A. MacDonald, *Korea: The War Before Vietnam* (New York: The Free Press, A Division of Macmillian, Inc., 1987), 176.

27. It speaks volumes to George Marshall's character that he urged Roosevelt to recall MacArthur after MacArthur had all but ended Marshall's career as a colonel. Pogue, *Organizer of Victory*, ix.

28. Eisenhower, *At Ease*, 213.

29. Stephen Ambrose, *Eisenhower, Volume Two, The President* (New York: Simon & Schuster, 1984), 104–107.

30. Admiral Arthur Radford, Memorandum, 31 March 1954, Ridgway Papers, U.S. Army Military History Institute, Carlisle Barracks, PA; Admiral Arthur Radford, recorded interview by Phillip A. Crowl, 8 May 1965, 46-50, the John Foster Dulles Oral History Project, Princeton University Library, Princeton, NJ.

31. Martin Windrow, *The Last Valley: Dien Bien Phu and the French Defeat in Vietnam* (Cambridge, MA: Da Capo Press, 2004), 565–566.

32. Ibid., 568. That contemplated use of nuclear weapons seems incredible now, but the early use of such weapons was both our government's policy and a key part of Eisenhower's New Look defense.

33. Matthew B. Ridgway, *SOLDIER: The Memoirs of Matthew B. Ridgway* (Harper & Brothers, New York, 1956). Lest we be too judgmental of the French, it is worth remembering that before Pearl Harbor, the draft that began the build-up of the U.S. Army in 1940 contained similar prohibitions on the use of American draftees overseas. Lingeman, *Don't You Know There's a War On?*, 19.

34. Ridgway, *Soldier*, 236.

35. Ibid., 278; General Matthew B. Ridgway, Memorandum, 21 April 1954, 17 May 1954, Ridgway Papers, U.S. Army Military History Institute, Carlisle Barracks, PA; "What Ridgway Told Ike," *U.S. News & World Report*, 25 June 1954, 30–32.

36. Kinnard, *Certain Trumpet*, 33.

37. General Maxwell D. Taylor, USA (Ret.), *The Uncertain Trumpet* (New York: Harper & Brothers, 1959), 28.

38. Michael Korda, *Ike: An American Hero* (New York: HarperCollins, 2007), 235.

39. Perret, *There's a War to Be Won*, 406.

40. Schwarzkopf, *It Doesn't Take a Hero*, 361–2.

41. General Ron Foggleman, USAF (Ret.).

42. 10 U.S. Code, Section 601.

43. This is now a widely held view, but I heard it best and most succinctly articulated by General Tony Zinni, USMC (Ret.), Armed Forces Day Dinner address, Louisville, Kentucky, 1999.

44. H.W. Brands, *Andrew Jackson, His Life and Times* (New York: Doubleday, 2005), 481.

CHAPTER 13

1. Winston S. Churchill, *The American Civil War* (New York: Fairfax Press, 1958). This volume was originally published as a part of Churchill's larger *History of the English Speaking Peoples*.

2. Manchester, *The Last Lion*, 19.

3. Kiron K. Skinner, Annelise Anderson, and Martin Anderson, *Reagan in His Own Hand: The Writings of Ronald Reagan that Reveal his Revolutionary Vision for America* (New York: Simon & Schuster, 2001).

4. David McCullough, *The Path Between the Seas: The Creation of the Panama Canal 1870-1914* (New York: Simon and Schuster, 1977), 245.

5. Edmund Morris, *The Rise of Theodore Roosevelt* (New York: Coward, McCann & Geoghegan, Inc, 1979,) 618–622.

6. Edmund Morris, *Theodore Rex* (New York: Random House, 2001), 6.

7. McCullough, *Path Between the Seas*, 257, 589.

8. Ibid., 407–409.

9. Edmund Morris, *Theodore Rex*, 502.

10. Eisenhower, *At Ease*, 378.

11. Perret, *There's a War to Be Won*, 300.

12. Franklin D. Roosevelt, Letter, 26 February 1942, George C. Marshall Research Foundation, Xerox 923, GCM-COAS-CO: Relationships, George C. Marshall Research Library, Lexington, Virginia.

13. http://www.cnn.com/video/#/video/politics/2007/10/13/starr.pace. vietnam.wall.notes.cnn ?iref=videosearch.

14. Lewis Sorley, *Thunderbolt: General Creighton Abrams and the Army of His Times* (New York: Simon & Schuster, 1992), 317.

15. Charles B. MacDonald, *A Time for Trumpets: The Untold Story of the Battle of the Bulge* (New York: Bantam Books, 1985), 529–532.

16. Sorley, *A Better War*, 17–18, 22, 42, 123–124.

17. Ibid., 217.

18. Edward J. Renehan, Jr., *The Lion's Pride, Theodore Roosevelt and His Family in Peace and War* (New York :Oxford UP, 1998), 127–129.

19. Manchester, *Last Lion*, 20.

CHAPTER 14

1. Lt. Gen. Harold G. Moore, USA (Ret.), and Joseph L. Galloway, *We Were Soldiers Once . . . And Young* (New York: Random House, 1992); After Action Report, Ia Drang Valley Operation, 9 Dec 1965; CJCS Lecture Series, Moore and Galloway, 2000.

2. Moore, *We Were Soldiers Once*, 199.

3. Lt. Gen. W.R. Peers, USA (Ret.), *The My Lai Inquiry* (New York: W.W. Norton & Co., 1979), 180.

4. Re: quarters, author was at Benning during that period. Re: parole, Peers, *The My Lai Inquiry*, 227.

5. Peers, *The My Lai Inquiry*, 3.

6. Wilbur Fisk Papers, Diary January–September 1864, 30 April 1864, Manuscript Division, Library of Congress, Washington, D.C.

7. Wilbur Fisk, *Hard Marching Every Day: The Civil War Letters of Private Wilbur Fisk, 1861-1865* (Lawrence, KS: UP of Kansas, 1992), 10, 88.

8. Fisk diary, 8 April 1863; Manuscript Division, Library of Congress, Washington, D.C.

9. Ibid., 4 May 1864.

10. Fisk, *Hard Marching* , 80.

11. Ibid., 116.

12. Fisk diary, 4 May 1864.

13. Wilbur Fisk Papers, 25.

14. Wilbur Fisk Papers, 28.

15. Alice Rains Trulock, *In the Hands of Providence: Joshua Lawrence Chamberlain and the American Civil War* (Chapel Hill, NC: The U of North Carolina Press, 1992), 181.

16. Gene Smith, *Lee and Grant: A Dual Biography* (New York: McGraw-Hill Book Company, 1987), 282; Brian Lamb, *Booknotes: Stories from American History* (New York: Penguin Books, 2001), 81.

CHAPTER 15

1. The Pentagon is trying to move to a more capabilities-based approach and away from the confines of a scenario approach. That is a step in the right direction, but someone still has to project what capabilities will be required.

2. The Confederate States of America was arguably another country: they had a constitution, borders, a government, an army, and a navy.

3. Goals, not to mention desperation, can overshadow values: for example, the United States/Soviet alliance in World War II.

Chapter 16

1. Forrest C. Pogue, *The United States Army in World War II: The European Theater of Operations, The Supreme Command* (Washington, D.C: Center of Military History, United States Army, 1996), Appendix E.
2. Ambrose, *Citizen Soldiers*, 56.
3. Ibid., 82.
4. Lingeman, *Don't You Know There's a War On?*, re: air defense surveillance, 50; re: civil defense workers, 59.
5. Ibid.,144.
6. Ibid., 288.
7. Ibid., 244.
8. The Allied strategic bombing campaigns in the European theater and in the Pacific have been questioned over the issue of civilian deaths.
9. Ambrose, *Citizen Soldiers*, 57.
10. Eisenhower letter to Marshall dated 15 April 1945, The Dwight D. Eisenhower Library, DDE/nmr: http://www.eisenhower.archives.gov/ dl/ holocaust/DDEtoGenMarshall15April45pg1-3.pdf.

Chapter 17

1. Bowen, *Miracle at Philadelphia*, 4.
2. Windrow, *Last Valley*, 431–432.
3. Sorley, *A Better War*, 370.

Index